IAN R MITCHELL was born in Aberdeen, spending his first 25 years in Torry and Kincorth. He graduated in History from Aberdeen University in 1973, following a couple of years working as a paper mill labourer and engineering machinist, and subsequently moved to Glasgow. Ian taught History at Clydebank College for over twenty years and whilst there wrote a standard textbook on *Bismarck and the Development of Germany*. He has written several books on mountaineering including the classic *Mountain Days & Bothy Nights* (1987), and *A View from the Ridge* (1991) (both co-authored with Dave Brown), the latter of which won the Boardman-Tasker Prize for Mountain Literature. More recently he has developed an interest in urban heritage and walking, and the recent fruits of this were *This City Now: Glasgow and its Working Class Past* (2005) and *Clydeside: Red, Orange and Green* (2009).

By the same Author

NON-FICTION

Mountain Days & Bothy Nights (1987) with Dave Brown
A View from the Ridge (1991, re-issued 2007) also with Dave Brown
Scotland's Mountains before the Mountaineers (1998)
On the Trail of Queen Victoria in the Highlands (2001)
Walking through Scotland's History (2000, re-issued 2007)
This City Now: Glasgow and its Working Class Past (2005)
Clydeside: Red, Orange and Green (2009)
Aberdeen Beyond the Granite (2010)
Prelude to Everest: Alexander Kellas, Himalayan Mountaineer (2011) with George W. Rodway

FICTION

Mountain Outlaw: Ewan MacPhee (2003)
Winter in Berlin, or The Mitropa Smile (2009)

A Glasgow Mosaic

Explorations Around the City's Urban Icons

IAN R MITCHELL

Luath Press Limited
EDINBURGH
www.luath.co.uk

First published 2013
Reprinted 2020

ISBN: 978-1-908373-66-3

The paper used in this book is recyclable. It is made from low chlorine pulps produced in a low energy, low emissions manner from renewable forests.

The publishers acknowledge the support of

towards the publication of this volume.

Printed and bound by
Bell & Bain Ltd., Glasgow

Typeset in 11 point Sabon
by 3btype.com

The author's right to be identified as author of this work under the Copyright, Designs and Patents Act 1988 has been asserted.

© Ian R Mitchell 2013

*I would like to dedicate this book to
Ann Laird of the Friends of Glasgow West,
and to Hunter Reid of the Maryhill Burgh Halls Trust,
two people who in their different ways have made
a solid contribution to Glasgow's Renaissance.*

Contents

Pre-Amble   9

CHAPTER ONE	Glasgow: Cinema City Reborn?	13
CHAPTER TWO	The Fabulous Factories File	23
CHAPTER THREE	Glasgow's Square Mile of Science	37
CHAPTER FOUR	A Measured Mile of Art	49
CHAPTER FIVE	Artistic Representations of Labour in Glasgow	59
CHAPTER SIX	Joan Eardley's Townhead	73
CHAPTER SEVEN	North Woodside: Iconography of a Forgotten Quarter	85
CHAPTER EIGHT	The Maryhill Panels: Stephen Adam's Stained Glass Workers	97
CHAPTER NINE	The Rise and Fall of the Old Govan Club: 1914–39	111
CHAPTER TEN	The Heart of Govan Beats Again	124
CHAPTER ELEVEN	Alex Ferguson's Govan	131
CHAPTER TWELVE	Metal Memorials: The Socialist City Centre	141
CHAPTER THIRTEEN	A Night at the Opry: an Evening Doon the Watter	151

Pre-Amble

THIS BOOK COMPLETES a trilogy of works begun in 2005 with *This City Now: Glasgow and its Working Class Past,* and continuing with *Clydeside: Red Orange and Green,* published in 2010. The three books have all had basically similar aims in trying to raise the profile of forgotten or neglected areas and aspects of Glasgow's and wider Clydeside's history – especially working class history – and thus in a small way to try and boost the esteem of the people who live in the locales covered, as well as to combat any possibly negative images held of these districts by outsiders. None of these books aim to be walking guidebooks, though to varying degrees in each chapter of each book there are enough directions and signposts for the reader to find his or her way around should they choose, as I hope they might, to leave their armchairs and exchange a virtual tour for the real thing. And neither are these essays meant to be, impossible anyway in the space given, full histories of these neglected districts. Rather, they represent my own personal encounters with the areas, enlivened and enriched, I hope, by my knowledge of the history they had undergone before I encountered them.

I have been wandering Glasgow's streets for over 40 years. Initially the aim I had was to inform myself about the city in which I had come to live and to educate myself by finding my way about its uncharted territories. As the years passed I realised I was living through a time of great and irreversible change in the city, and was witnessing the ultimate stages of its de-industrialisation, with the attendant social and economic issues raised by that process. I began to record this transformation in notes and images for myself. Then, as the city began its renaissance as a City of Culture, and interest in its present and past increased, I thought it would be useful to write about Glasgow, about its history and about my own personal encounters with that history for any others who wished to actually go walkabout, on virtual or real journeys, off its beaten tracks and rat runs.

It was only later that I realised I was following a trodden path, and that there was a long tradition of urban walking stretching back to those who explored the London streets from the late 18th century onwards, writers such as Blake, De Quincey and Stevenson. As cities grew in size in the 19th century, they became unfamiliar wildernesses, peopled by dangerous tribes (the Parisian underclass were designated 'Apaches'). The city became a new frontier, and, as the French poet Charles Baudelaire said, 'what are the dangers of the forest and the prairie, compared with the daily shocks and conflicts of civilisation'. In *Paris Spleen*, Baudelaire imagined the urban wanderer as follows:

> The crowd is his element, as the air is that of the birds and water of fishes. His passion and his profession are to become one flesh with the crowd. For the perfect *flaneur*, for a passionate spectator, it is an immense joy to set up house in the heat of the multitude, amid the ebb and flow of movement, in the midst of the fugitive and the infinite. To be away from home and yet to find oneself everywhere at home; to see the world, to be at the centre of the world, and yet to remain hidden from the world...

Paris especially became the urban walker's homeland, with such writers as André Breton and the exiled German thinker Walter Benjamin roaming its streets, the latter theorising in *Reflections*, about the meaning of the urban landscape:

> Not to find one's way in a city may well be uninteresting and banal... But to lose oneself in a city – as one loses oneself in a forest – that calls for quite a different schooling. The signboards and street names, passers-by, roofs, kiosks or bars, must speak to the wanderer like the cracking twig under his feet, like the startling call of a bittern in the distance, like the sudden stillness of a clearing with a lily standing erect at its centre. Paris taught me this art of straying.

Between them these quotations illustrate respectively the learning process undergone by the urban walker – who has to know where to look and what to look for – and the intense pleasure such an activity brings to the engaged and informed observer. And you can experience this learning, and this pleasure in any large city, not just London – or Paris.

Over the past decade or more there has been an explosion of writing and theorising about this phenomenon of urban walking which has emerged as the subject of a new academic discipline, taking on the name psychogeography – a phrase coined by the French writer Guy Debord half a century ago. There are writing careers and academic posts in psychogeography now. But in this process urban walking appears to me to have lost a little of its edge, and to have headed towards a certain narcissism. Many studies from this school of thought appear to indicate that their authors spent their time not actually on the streets, but in libraries and archives reading other psychogeographers past and present, and addressing their written productions not towards a wider audience, but towards these, their peers. The books produced are often more about what is going on inside the head of the observer than outside of it in the social streetscape.

In trying to avoid this pitfall, I am pleased that through the writing of these books I have come involved in giving talks to, and leading walks for, both local people and visitors, in many of the areas concerned. I have also been involved in a modest way in helping with various social, community and heritage projects in Maryhill, Govan and elsewhere in the city. More than with any other works I have written, these books of urban wanderings have made a modest connection with their audience in a practical and interactive way, which is deeply gratifying.

A century ago, Glasgow was one of the ten largest cities in Europe, the only non-capital city (apart from Naples) which had over 1,000,000 people. In keeping with this, it has built a legacy which the authoritative *The Buildings of Scotland: Glasgow* by Elizabeth Williamson, Anne Riches and Malcolm Higgs (2005), describes as follows:

> A visitor with time to spare will find that the city centre is rich with remarkable buildings from the height of its industrial prosperity and that the grandest suburbs are planned on a scale comparable with many European capitals.

That much is now widely accepted, but the claim to greatness of the city goes further than its built heritage, encompassing as it does a much broader range of creative output. When we compare its contribution with that of other non-capital cities of a similar built size with regard to historical-cultural legacy, we can see that Glasgow has punched far above its relative weight. No city of comparable dimension has had a world impact of comparable measure, in economic, social and artistic terms, Looking at possible rivals, where is Glasgow's peer? Birmingham? Lyon? Turin? Hamburg? Posing the question answers it.

Barcelona may have its Gaudi to rival Mackintosh, but where is its Watt, is Kelvin? Outside of the capital cities – and not all of these – nowhere suggested can match the overall rounded contribution to 'culture' in its broadest sense, that Glasgow has had in the past two centuries or more. To try and demonstrate this was one of the aims I had in writing this book. The gauntlet is on the ground, I would be interested to see who attempts to pick it up.

Ian Mitchell, 2013

CHAPTER ONE

Glasgow: Cinema City Reborn?

IT IS SOMETIMES said that if an Edinburgher has a pound, he or she will save it, but that if a Glaswegian has a pound, they will go out and spend it. When one looks at the vast crowds in Glasgow that patronise football matches, or went to the dancing in its heyday, there would appear to be at least a grain of truth in this statement. It is given further credence by the statistics of cinema attendance in its classic period 1920–60, when the term 'Cinema City' was often applied to Glasgow due to the huge number of cinemas located there and the large audiences they boasted. In 1950 the district of Govan alone had nine cinemas, one more than the entire city of Aberdeen, which was home to twice Govan's population.

During this classic period of cinema, Glasgow itself hardly featured on the silver screen, except in a few documentaries such as the 1960 *Seawards the Great Ships*, directed by Hilary Harris. This was written by John Grierson and Cliff Hanley and showed the Clyde shipyards at the height of their post-war reconstruction boom. It was the first Scottish film to be awarded an Oscar. But now the reel appears to have come full circle, and Cinema City has been re-born as a place where, increasingly, feature films are actually made. Glasgow itself has become a movie star. The city's universities now have prestigious Film Studies courses on offer, and the facilities for making movies in the city are world class, such as the Film City unit located in the former Govan Town Hall. In recognition of this, the City Council has created a dedicated Film Office to promote the use of Glasgow as a film location. Whilst it is not yet Hollywood on the Clyde, the film industry is one of the growing economic sectors in the Glasgow region, worth an estimated £25 million a year.

Many of these recent films have featured Glasgow as Elsewhere. In Terence Davies' *The House of Mirth*, the city doubled for late-19th-century New York, with the tenements of Hillhead and Woodlands acting as stand-ins for those of the Lower East Side a century before, and Alexander Thomson's Great Western Terrace doubling as the homes of the New York plutocracy. The city's Moss Heights housing project has been Moscow, Rome has been recreated with the City Chambers as the Vatican, and the steep streets of Partick have doubled as those of San Francisco. The great variety of architectural styles in Glasgow allows this transformation to happen. Few places have such an eclectic built environment within so manageable an area; it is, for obvious reasons, a director's delight. A recent example of Glasgow as Elsewhere was the filming of *World War Z,* starring Brad Pitt, with Glasgow serving as Philadelphia facing a zombie invasion.

Because Glasgow can be Elsewhere, it can also be Nowhere. It is not a city in which you might consider setting an urban version of *Brigadoon*. It has, at times, a stark grimness, and this allows it to be used as an imaginary place and the setting for dystopian studies of urban and social breakdown, such as in *Death Watch*. This is my favourite film set in Glasgow, indeed one of my all-time favourite films, which I saw on its first release over 30 years ago. Then it was a total flop, despite boasting an A-List cast which included Harvey Keitel and Romy Schneider, but it has just been re-released to what I am certain will be a much better reception. Bertrand Tavernier, *Death Watch*'s director, came to the Glasgow Film Festival in 2012 to launch its re-release. Tavernier described how he fell in love with Glasgow and its people back in the 1970s, and how he has been here many times since. He talked of the filming of *Death Watch* (despite the warnings he had had that the film crews would be robbed and mugged) as the easiest shoot he has ever done, and of the enthusiastic help and participation offered by local people. The film describes an imaginary future in which reality television looms over every waking moment of our lives. A grim vision, Tavernier thought it would remain an unrealised science-fiction fantasy, but in many ways it has actually arrived, as has the time of this very prescient film.

Late 1970s Glasgow; the slums still standing, black as night and unoccupied, is the setting for this future. The poor live on the city margins, held down by the authorities, and the middle classes lead lives where death by illness has been abolished and where intrusive, commercially-driven reality television dominates people's existence. The city has never been portrayed as dramatically, or in such tones of brooding beauty, as in *Death Watch*. From shots of the Necropolis (then still wild and unprettified), to scenes by the riverside (which at that time still had ships at the docks), it captures a dark side of the city to startling effect.

My main interest, though, is not in Glasgow as Elsewhere, or even as Nowhere, but as itself. How have directors, producers and script writers portrayed the city in what is essentially its period of post-industrial development, its City of Culture period, following upon the industrial greatness of *Second City* and then the urban decline of *No Mean City*? What aspects and issues have attracted their interest, and how representative is the view of the city which they have given? Let us first look at what these works do *not* concentrate on.

Death Watch promotional poster for its re-release. A prescient account of the horrors of 'reality' television. (*Park Circus*).

There have been almost no historical films made about the city, set in its rich and varied past or in its industrial and commercial heyday, which lasted till the early 20th century. This may change as Glasgow's film profile rises, but to date, the only full length film about Glasgow set in a historical context is David Lean's *Madeleine* from 1950, based on the true story of a young woman's attempt to challenge the strict bourgeois values of the mid-19th-century. As this was a studio production, the city was literally a stage backdrop, and this backdrop full of inaccuracies. Madeleine's lover lived in a replica Edinburgh High Street slum, when in reality he occupied a bourgeois flat in Argyle Street. Wild Highlanders partied at the Smith family's holiday house... in Helensburgh. The list goes on. But historically accurate *mise en scene* was not Lean's interest; Madeleine's drama was.

Historical is possibly a strong word to apply to *Young Adam*. Directed by David Mackenzie in 2003 and starring Ewan MacGregor, it depicts life in industrial Glasgow and its environs around 1950, as seen through the work of bargees on the Forth and Clyde canal, a life and a world that has almost totally disappeared in the ensuing half-century. We can thus be forgiven for using the term here. Documenting the claustrophobic and conformist society of the time from which the young writer Joe wishes to escape, the director encountered a fundamental problem in capturing the industrial environs of the canal from half a century ago: they are simply no longer there. In fact, the Forth and Clyde canal was re-opened early this century as a leisure, cultural and environmental project, reflecting changed times. To blot out these changes, much of the film was shot in bad weather (no problem in Glasgow!) and with the background out of focus, so that, for example, the warehouses at Spiers Wharf could still look like warehouses, and not the luxury flats they have become.

I would make my first plea for film makers to use Glasgow's past more than they have as a future subject for their works. From the Covenanters and Jacobites to the Tobacco Lords, from the Industrial Revolution to blockade running during the US Civil War – the choice of topics is almost endless!

One special omission, given that Glasgow is and has been a working-class city and the crucible of the Scottish labour movement, is that the working class and its struggles have not featured on film, either in historical or contemporary times, apart from in documentaries. An obvious and worthwhile film topic, heretofore ignored entirely by the film industry, would be the Red Clydeside period around the First World War and the life of the great Glasgow socialist John MacLean. But there are many more potential topics available. The atmosphere which surrounded the UCS Work-In is retreating into history to such an extent that it could also offer scope for imaginative cinematic treatment.

But unfortunately, what sells Glasgow is its *No Mean City* image. It is therefore surprising that the best-selling and most famous work of fiction on Glasgow, the novel of that title by Alexander McArthur which was set in 1930s Gorbals, has never itself been made into a film. In the last 30 years the marginalised and excluded of the city, first captured by McArthur, must have become one of the most over-documented fauna on the planet. I have no problem with the issue of Glasgow's poverty and violence being given attention – quite the contrary, I would hate to see it airbrushed, or soft-focussed, its existence denied – I do, however, have an issue with this being projected, almost to the exclusion of the mainstream life of the city, as the paradigm of the place. There have been exceptions. Think of the TV dramatization of John Byrne's *Tutti Frutti*, which virtually launched the careers of Emma Thompson and Robbie Coltrane. It charted the problems of a group of edgy, marginal (but not socially excluded) musicians in the mid-1980s with great warmth, humour and sadness, and was set in a Glasgow that showed the scars of its past alongside the emerging Culture City. But too much of the film coverage of Glasgow in the last couple of decades could be described as Miserabilist.

The first really outstanding and internationally successful Scottish feature film director was Bill Forsyth. Sadly, after making the successful *Local Hero* in 1983 (which featured Burt Lancaster, then at the height of his career, who was BAFTA-nominated for his role),

Forsyth departed for Hollywood where, many would argue, he experienced an atrophy of his talents. Before that he made a cluster of films set in Glasgow and its environs which dealt with the then newly emerging problems of unemployment and social marginalisation. Films such as *That Sinking Feeling, Gregory's Girl* (set in Cumbernauld, a bit of Glasgow overspill sited on a windy hill) and *Comfort and Joy* deftly captured the pitfalls of urban life without denying its corresponding benefits. The latter film, which starred Glasgow's own Bill Patterson, portrayed, with Forsyth's unique brand of whimsy and banter, the origins of the so-called 'Ice-Cream Wars' of that period on the Glasgow housing estates.

What is surprising in rewatching these films is that there is no despair in them. The kids in Forsyth's films are healthy, reasonably-dressed and optimistic; when one character in *That Sinking Feeling* says 'there must be mair tae life than suicide', he means it. It isn't a statement of despair, but one of optimism. There were no drugs in these kids' lives, and there was little violence. Even the feuding gangs in the Ice-Cream Wars of *Comfort and Joy* spray each other with raspberry juice. Some argue that Forsyth was casting a rosy glow on his image of Glasgow at that period. Violence was an issue even then, and indeed, shortly after the comic hi-jinks of the Ice Cream Wars in *Comfort and Joy* appeared, large scale thuggery broke out as Ice Cream vans in the peripheral housing estates became the carriers of drugs, heralding the onset of organised gangsterism and its attendant brutalities. These tensions certainly simmered beneath the surface of Forsyth's film but, in casting his battles as acts of comedic absurdity, he developed a broader portrait of Glasgow's human side that was unburdened by the grim realities of such smaller social pockets, allowing the city a dimension of warmth that is denied by too many. The warm-hearted whimsy and cheering banter that characterised Forsyth's films did not altogether vanish from Scottish cinema, and in 2002 there appeared a film which readers of *The List* magazine voted one of the three best Scottish films of all time. *American Cousins*, like *Comfort and Joy*, is set in the Italian community of Glasgow, though in its fish and chip rather than its ice-cream sub-culture, which its director Don Coutts portrays with perhaps a pinch more accuracy than Forsyth did, as those familiar with this most successfully integrated immigrant community will testify. The film deals with the issues of gangsterism, poverty and urban decay, but with an uplifting humanity that produces a wonderful feel-good factor. The city is nicely showcased, with icons such as the former Luma Works and its riverscapes – even its urban wastelands – shown to be a thing of staggering beauty. *The List* readers might agree with my own love of this film, but to the wider public, it remains little known.

Glasgow's film profile rose meteorically when the renowned director Ken Loach fell in love with the city, engaged, like Tavernier before him, by both the energy and humour of its inhabitants and the dramatic possibilities offered for filming in myriad locations in and around the city. Films like *Sweet Sixteen* and *My Name is Joe* were international successes for the director and brought Glasgow and Clydeside to a wider audience. Glasgow native Peter Mullen, who had starred in the latter film and in others such as *On a Clear Day*, then went on to direct his own films in a similar genre: *Orphans*, and, most recently, *Neds*, set in the Glasgow of the 1970s. Where one might argue that Forsyth underplayed social problems in his films, it could also be argued that Loach and Mullen overplayed them. Glasgow gangs of the 1970s certainly existed, but not to the extent dreamed up by sociologists at the time. Loach himself has recently taken a leaf out of Forsyth's book, creating films that appeal on a feel good level. His most recent work, *Angel's Share*, is a redemptive drama about a group of unemployed Glasgow kids who go on a whisky heist. The world in which their tale takes place is a more brutal one than that portrayed by Forsyth 30 years before, but the comedic heart still beats at its core.

Generally, though, it is Miserabilism that still dominates cinematic images of Glasgow. A bleak misery certainly directs much of Andrea Arnold's stylish thriller from 2006, *Red Road*, named after the mega-rise flats of that name (now in the process of being demolished) on the edge of the Springburn area of the city. A well-cast and gripping film which won the Jury Prize at the Cannes Film Festival,

Red Road does nothing, however, to combat the misleading and widespread image that Glasgow consists of little more than alienated urban wastelands. With its rich history, wonderfully varied built heritage and current cultural renaissance, Glasgow deserves better from the silver screen than that.

Cinema should certainly not forget the middle classes. The West End of Glasgow has a population of well over 100,000 people. It is a city-within-a-city, with a built environment equivalent to that of any European capital, and where reputedly there are more University graduates as a proportion of the population than anywhere else in the UK, and where health and wealth statistics are far from those of the Death by Deep Fried Mars Bar image of the Dear Green Place so beloved of cosmopolitan scribblers. Though these social groups have featured in a couple of television drama serialisations, most notably *The Book Group* (dealing with the mores of a group of Byres Road would-be *literati*) and *Lip Service* (about a group of professional lipstick-lesbians, though that was set in the detached West End colony of the Merchant City), they have yet to feature on film.

There have thus been few, if any, attempts to follow up on Lean's account of the 19th-century Glasgow middle class in *Madeleine*. A possible exception might be made for the 2002 film *Wilbur (Wants to Kill Himself)*, directed by Lone Sherfig. This was an almost entirely Danish-written and directed film, but set in Glasgow (as Glasgow) with a Scottish cast! It deals with a pair of brothers running a struggling second-hand bookshop, and despite its title it is a film which treats suicide, death and loss in a beautifully uplifting way, without any *schmaltz* – and also without any Miserabilism!

If Glasgow has a future as a Cinema City – as opposed to just a wonderfully chameleon-like location for films set Elsewhere – it can only be by widening the topics which have dominated the films of the last 30 years, and by providing us with a more accurate portrait of the city in its past and its present. Miserabilism may currently sell, but the cinema-going public will eventually tire of it. Broaden the social canvas, broaden the historical dimension. There is more material there than there is oil in the North Sea. In the chapters which follow I hope to be able to present a picture of Glasgow, a city which may be cinematically rooted in an image of Miserabilism, but which has in reality been a launch pad for an incredible wealth of intellectual and human culture of an intensely positive nature.

Much fascinating information on the history of cinema in Glasgow (and elsewhere) can be found on the Scottish cinemas and theatres project's website

http://www.scottishcinemas.org.

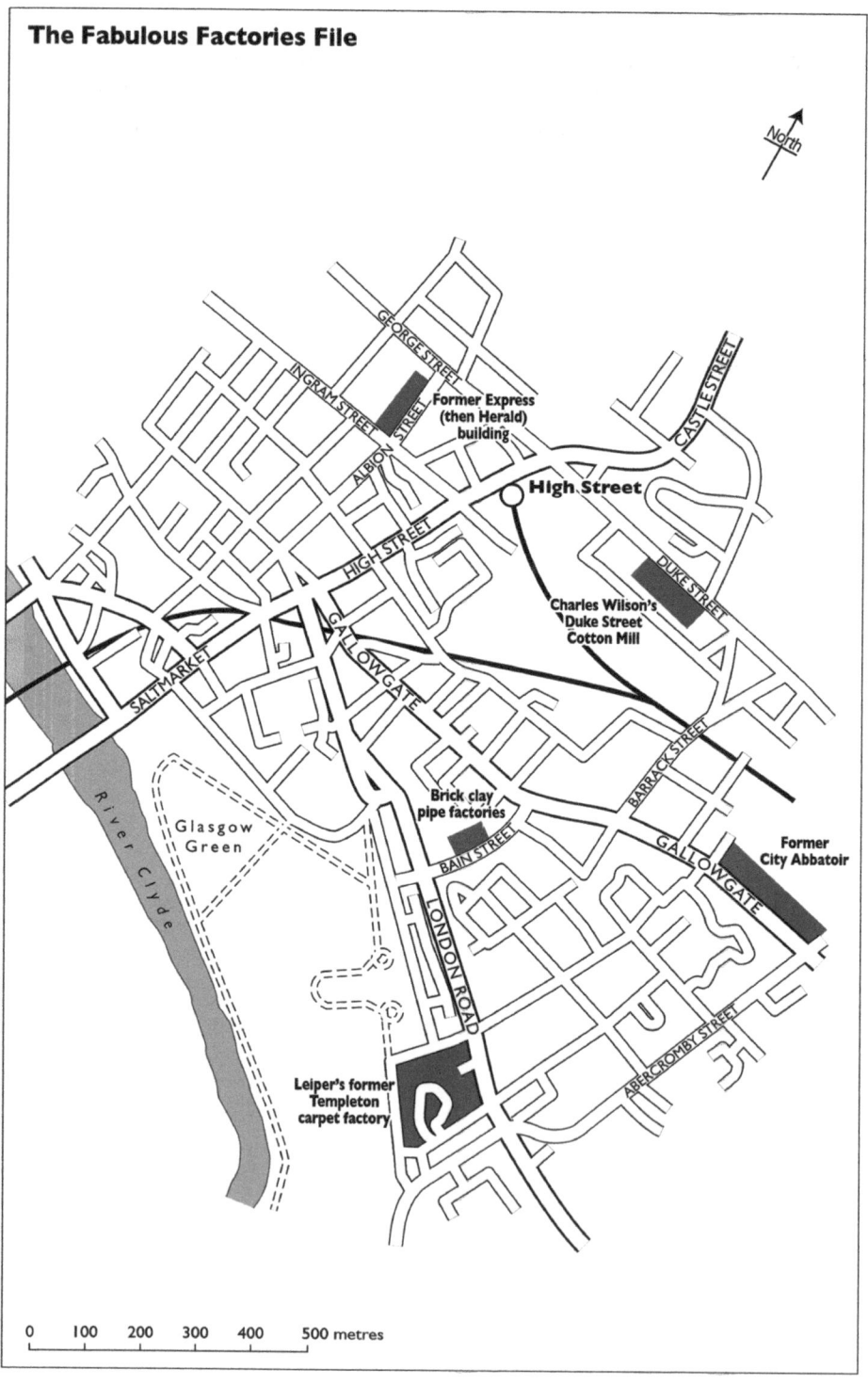

CHAPTER TWO

The Fabulous Factories File

THE WORD 'FACTORY' has acquired mostly negative connotations over the past two centuries. Just as 'tenement' came to be linked with the idea of slum housing, so 'factory' has developed an association (from the time of William Blake's blast in his poem *Jerusalem* against the 'Dark Satanic Mills' of the Industrial Revolution) with ugliness on the outside and unpleasant things going on inside. Whilst we have gradually come to realise that other monuments of the industrial era, such as railway stations and canal aqueducts, are often things of staggering beauty, there has been a much slower shift in our perception of industrial buildings, many of which, until recently, stood begrimed and disused, regarded mostly as suitable cases for demolition and landscape clearance.

It would be pointless to claim that all, or even most, of the factories built in the two centuries of Scotland's industrial era were creations of architectural merit. Architectural flair, ornamentation and expenses were largely devoted to the stately homes of the aristocracy and gentry, or to the town halls and suburban villas built by the urban bourgeoisie in Victorian times, for obvious reasons. Many industrial buildings were erected quickly, out of the cheapest materials available and with no regard for aesthetic value other than the beauty of the profit-sheet which they were expected to generate. However, there are numerous exceptions to this, and these exceptions have left us with a generally under-appreciated legacy of striking industrial buildings in Scotland. Much of this legacy lies on Clydeside, and especially in Glasgow, where most of the examples in this chapter are located.

Many of the best architects of the industrial age were Glasgow-based, and several of them designed factories and tenements as well as civic and ecclesiastic buildings. The city's enthusiasm for creative flair, shared even by some of the hard-headed businessmen driving its industrial explosion, is responsible for a concentration of industrial buildings of a quality and a variety lacking elsewhere in its riparian hinterland, or indeed throughout the rest of Scotland and even possibly in the whole UK. It gives the city a visual identity which is easily comparable with the industrial archaeology of the wider world. How did it come about that buildings whose purpose was primarily utilitarian were often of exceptional aesthetic quality? As the following chapter articulates, the reasons were varied and manifold.

Sometimes a capitalist would be of the philanthropic mould and would devote more than a functional concern to the construction of his workplace, motivated by a benevolent regard for the welfare of his workforce. In other circumstances, the industrialist wanted to make his workplace – or at least the administrative part of it – a statement of his grandeur and economic intentions, to impress customers and upset rivals. Then there were those entrepreneurs who, dazzled by the success of industrial advance in general, wished to incorporate the latest technology and materials into the construction of their enterprise, or even, as we shall see, to use the very building itself to advertise what was produced within it.

In Scotland we are especially favoured, by comparison with many parts of our southern neighbour, in that the building material for the early factories was most often stone. The wide availability of accessible stone – especially of the easily worked sandstone in west-central Scotland – meant that, unlike in the industrial cities of northern England, where the main building material was brick, in Scotland the durability and aesthetic appeal of many factories was enhanced by the material of their construction. Steam power, which was applied to the cutting of sandstone from the 1830s onwards, reduced the cost of building in stone and made the material financially viable for general factory construction. Although most of the early factories were erected by companies whose most professional employee would have been a master-mason with little or no architectural background, there was a template to hand for them to use in factory design. Until about 1850, a large proportion of early industry was rural, due to the easy availability of water power, and many of the factories constructed were moderate, less ornate copies of the Palladian mansions which could be seen throughout rural Scotland. The fact that in so many small Scottish former textile towns their old factories are converted to workspaces – and even dwellings – testifies not only to their durability, but also to their inherent aesthetic appeal.

The impressive mills and housing which can be found at New Lanark were not built by a member of the famous Adam mansion-building dynasty, but they certainly look as if they could have been. The construction is classical, perhaps even severe, with some limited ornamentation provided by detailing around doors and window frames, especially in focal corners or central buildings. The whole complex is so well built that, after over 200 years, almost all of the original buildings still stand and most continue to be used in a variety of forms. Many of the tenements have been remodelled into provide modern housing. There is a Youth Hostel and a contemporary hotel in one of the former mill buildings, and the whole site has been designated a UNESCO World Heritage Site. Behind these Palladian buildings lay the Enlightenment ideas of rationality and progress and the search for 'improvement' in the human condition, exemplified so well by the ideas of Dale and more especially of Robert Owen with his 'New View of Society'. Their aesthetic value evinces the 19th-century belief that human character was determined by social conditions.

The change in our ways of seeing older industrial building is clear, should we look at Spiers Wharf in Glasgow. As late as the 1980s there stood a collection of soot-encrusted warehouses and former grain and sugar mills in disrepair, 20 years after the closure of the Forth and Clyde Canal, at whose Glasgow branch terminus the buildings lay. Despite their mid-19th-century construction, their appearance is similar to the buildings at New Lanark. 'Late Palladian' might be an appropriate description of the style. The buildings underwent a variety of industrial uses before being converted into flats and offices, complete with a canal-side restaurant. They are stunningly eye-catching when lit up at night and seen from the M8 motorway. But how many who admire them today would have argued against their demolition 30 years ago, when theirs was nothing more than a crumbling industrial facade?

A similar story can be told of the Duke Street Cotton Mill, which was designed and built in the Italian Renaissance style in 1849 by Charles Wilson, one of Glasgow's leading architects at the time. Wilson built many of Glasgow's finest mansions and churches during the High Victorian period, including those of the Park Circus area where much of Glasgow's upper classes then lived, but he also turned his hand to tenements and factories. The Duke Street factory was later converted to the Great Eastern Hotel, causing many to think it was built thus for the nearby High Street railway goods terminal. In reality its conversion to a working man's hostel came 60 years after it was constructed by Wilson as one of the first fireproof factories. However, not only has this 'outstanding industrial building' (John Hume: *Industrial Archaeology of Glasgow*, 1974) been converted into dwellings, but the line of Duke Street has also been maintained and enhanced by the extension eastwards of the project into new, sympathetically matching housing built alongside the original building.

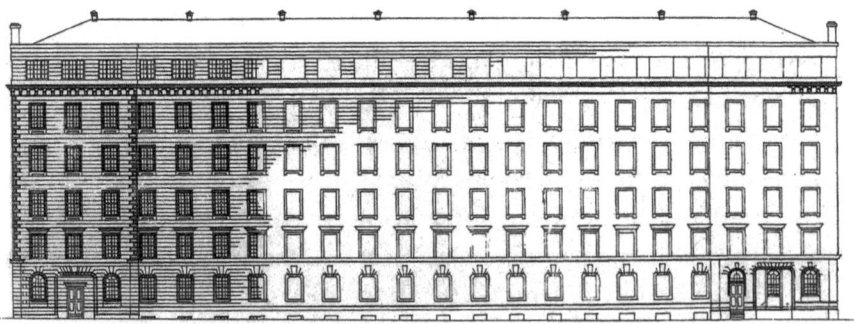

The aesthetically pleasing, classical lines of Wilson's Duke Street Cotton Mill explain why many thought it had been built for residential rather than industrial purposes.

The movement of industry to urban areas, made possible by the arrival of the steam engine in the late 18th century coupled with the development of a Scottish brick industry, meant that the proportion of factories which were stone-built decreased, and stone was increasingly only used for office construction while the production buildings were rendered in brick or other materials. Cast iron, and later steel-framed building, also encouraged construction in brick; stone could support itself without interior metal framing, whereas brick could not. With increasing demand for general house building, and supplies requiring transportation from ever further way, stone was increasing in cost as a building material as the 19th century progressed.

The aesthetic appeal of brick built factories does not rival that of those constructed in stone. However, some of the new brick-built factories were not without visually pleasing qualities, such as the charming Calton Clay Pipe Factory on Bain Street, the delightful smart facades of which were completed in 1876. A cast-iron frame supports the pair of red and yellow brick towers with their arched windows and bay centrepieces. This French Renaissance work was originally planned to be stone-built, but downgraded to brick, a sign of the fact that, for some capitalists, stone added a cost too high by this time. The original site lies in the heart of Glasgow's own *souk*, the Barras Market, but the buildings have since been converted to flats. Other architects – such as James Salmon, who also laid out the (originally) prestigious residential suburb of Dennistoun – varied the format of brick construction by using coloured polychrome bricks and designing a Venetian style frontage at his Kingston Grain Mills; sadly this building has been demolished. The increasing sophistication of the brick industry meant that new materials were constantly coming onto the market and products such as glazed bricks and coloured bricks found favour, whilst the cheapening in production of ceramic tiles associated with house building led to architects experimenting with these materials.

To add a touch of irony, in Victorian Glasgow, sandstone city *par excellence*, what is probably the most fabulous – and certainly the most beautiful – factory in the city, one which can have few rivals throughout the world, has its astounding frontage largely built in brick, though not 'red brick' as we know it. This is Templeton's carpet factory on Glasgow Green. The leading architect William Leiper designed this frontage to the works in the 1880s. Sandstone is used for the statues and the dressings around the windows and at the corners of the building, but the rest is an extravaganza of polychrome brick, glazed tiles, vitreous enamel mosaic and terracotta. It is constructed in a Gothic Revival, Ruskinesque style with architectural quotations from the Doge's Palace in Venice. This frontage did not support anything, and was fixed to the main factory building behind. What we see today is the second version, which dates from 1892, as the first had collapsed during construction in 1889, killing 29 female textile workers. Much of the building, along with its sympathetic additions from the 1950s – which were built with similar materials to the original building but in a late Art Deco style – has been converted to housing with the rest hosting offices, a gym and a micro-brewery.

Most of the best factories, however, continued to be built in stone. New hydraulic tools dating from around 1880 meant that the mason was freed from his hammer and chisel, and that the later Victorian factories could afford to indulge in the ornamentation that was the fashion of the time, moving away from the clean-lined classicism of the earlier 19th century into Gothic Revival and Art Nouveau styles. Factories began, like public buildings, to be ornamented with allegorical figures, with images of the products they produced or even – though much more rarely – with representations of the workers who laboured within them. Not to be left behind were the Glasgow City Fathers, whose standard of work, exemplified in public buildings, was consistently high. Though largely building facilities like the Corporation Fish Market, which were not strictly factories, one civic building they constructed, the Public Abattoir, was a factory in all but name, a production line churning out the daily needs of the city for meat. Designed in 1875 by John Carrick, the City Architect, the actual abattoir is built from iron and brick, but the entrances to the meat and cattle markets are triumphal sandstone Roman archways, adorned with reliefs of animals' heads and fine cast iron gates. Built on the site of a failed Regency housing development, the area is again being redeveloped as housing following the closure of the abattoir after a century of use.

Also built in stone, though it would be hard to tell at first glance, is Walter Macfarlane's Saracen Foundry in Possilpark. This must have been, in its day, one of the most fabulous factories of all – though possibly not corresponding with everyone's idea of beauty. It was demolished in 1967, two years short of its centenary, and not even a photograph of it apparently remains, though an illustration from a *Macfarlane's Castings* Victorian business catalogue gives us some idea of the building. James Boucher, a great Glasgow architect of the day, built Macfarlane's mansion in Glasgow's Park Circus. Boucher also built the Saracen Foundry, probably one of the few – if not the only – examples in the world faced with cast-iron, the products of Macfarlane's own workplace, whose output the factory

Macfarlane's Possil Ironworks
A neo-Gothic cast-iron clad extravaganza, as likely to impress any potential customer as Macfarlane's business catalogue.

frontage itself advertised. The chimneys were topped with cast-iron, the central cupola was clad with metal in abundance, and the roof was balustraded with it. The elaborate door surrounds sported the material, and, of course, the cast-iron downpipes and gutters added a final touch. What a draw to visitors to the city it could have been, had it survived! It was a unique example of an industrial facility that was actually advertising its own products in its construction and design.

Glasgow's shipbuilding and locomotive industries were the two main pillars of the city's prosperity in the later 19th century, and the capitalists in 19th-century Govan and Springburn, where the undertakings were respectively located, produced many buildings worthy of the glorious ships and trains they manufactured for the world. As befits what was for decades the biggest and most advanced shipyard in the world, the office block built in the late 1880s for Fairfield shipyard by the company Keppie Architects has been described as the most opulent in existence. It is Italian Renaissance in style, with a temple front containing a large staircase window, and adorned by nautical carved motifs of mermaids and sea gods, as well as a unique pair of shipyard workers. The interior is equally luxurious. After a long period standing empty, the building is being redeveloped into workspaces as part of the regeneration of central Govan. The actual shipyard itself, operated by BAE Systems, is still in operation, in large part due to the UCS Work-In of 1971–72, which had its focus here in Fairfield's.

Most of Glasgow's locomotive builders merged into the North British Locomotive Company in 1903, who shortly thereafter built their new offices in Springburn. The interior, with large stained glass World War One memorials adorning the main staircase, and the Board Room, with its stunning plasterwork and balcony, outdoes even the Fairfield offices in Govan. Indeed, there is so much to see in this building that it boasts its own heritage trail. The exterior of the building, designed by James Miller, is in the English baroque style. A cartouche above the doorway shows a North British Atlantic locomotive with chains and haulage gear as if emerging from the building, and figures of Speed and Science (as was typical then, depicted as idealised maidens) flank this centrepiece. Fine cast-iron work and granite pillars complete this most impressive of entrances. Glasgow's locomotive-building industry ended in 1962 and the office-block was converted into a college. After lying vacant for some time, it is now being utilised as workspace units, but it appears to be struggling in that new role. Development as housing would be extremely expensive and, given Springburn's unfashionable location, would probably be unappealing to a property developer in today's economic climate.

Last, but certainly not least, in the over-the top Beaux Arts style of highly ornamented factory frontages, is the Argyll Motor Company's offices in Alexandria, sitting to the west of Glasgow. The extravagance of this Edwardian building helped bankrupt the company in less than a decade. The exterior of carved sandstone figures, granite columns and two large globes with a motor car relief is as extravagant as the interior, which features, amongst other things, a marble staircase, marble pillars and French wall-tiling. After the collapse of the Argyll Motor Company the works became the Government's torpedo factory, then a manufacturing unit for Plessey, before the last industrial occupant quit in the 1980s. Now the building is a flagging retail outlet, much of it unoccupied. There would appear to be a limit to the amount of work and retail space currently needed, given the financial crisis on a national scale.

When discussing styles of factory buildings, it is notable that very few factories, to my knowledge, were constructed in the Art Nouveau style, a style which in many ways rejected industrialism for an idealised pre-industrial 'arts and crafts' outlook. It is interesting to speculate what a Rennie Mackintosh factory would have looked like – we can perhaps glean some idea from a fascinating design for a railway station he produced, but which was never realised. Possibly the only local exception to this rule was the printing works built for the art publishers Miller and Lang in Pollokshields by DB Dobson in 1903. This was constructed in the Glasgow Style – the local variant of Art Nouveau made popular by visionaries such as Mackintosh – both as regards the exterior and the interior.

This extravaganza of Gothic Revival and Beaux Arts factories faltered even before the outbreak of war in 1914. New styles and new materials, prefiguring the 1920s and 1930s, were becoming popular in factory construction. The most significant of these was concrete, which was already replacing stone and brick in many major construction projects (for instance MacAlpine's Glenfinnan railway viaduct). Many architects decided that this was the material of the future and designed whole factories built of re-enforced concrete, also using new features such as cast-steel window frames. Even before World War One, Glasgow had a pioneering example of this in the Jessie Street factory in Polmadie. Notable in other ways as 'the only shipyard on dry land', the works prefabricated small craft that would later be assembled on-site worldwide. The architect was Glasgow-born Archie Leitch, who built many pre-WWII football stadia in Britain, including Rangers FC's Ibrox Stadium. He also built factories, of which Jessie Street – from 1903 – is of great significance, being one of the first in the world to be constructed of re-enforced concrete. Currently derelict and used primarily as a venue for car-boot sales, this neglected historic building, if restored, could resemble another nearby building constructed of the same material and integrated much more successfully into modern Glasgow: Weir's of Cathcart. This was erected in 1912 to a design bought as a package from the USA-based Kahn's Trussed Concrete Steel Co., the firm who had built the Packard auto factory in Detroit. Concrete infill panels were used instead of brick in an example of uncompromising modernism. Weir believed the future lay in American-style factory design and American-style working practises, and his attempts to introduce these led to a series of strikes in the highly-unionised Cathcart works. The factory is one of the few large-scale industrial units left in Glasgow. Weir's recently tried to close it down and sell it for a housing development, but this plan fortunately fell through, and the new owners are continuing the tradition of manufacturing high quality pumps in Cathcart for a worldwide market.

Another modernist factory from the same period which shows the influence of European architecture is the former North British

Diesel Engine Works in Scotstoun, once part of the now long-closed Barclay, Curle and Co. shipyard. The architect, Karl Bernhardt, had worked with Peter Behrens on the AEG turbine factory in Berlin a few years previously, and this is clearly reflected in the distinctive and still visible Germanic mansard roof of the steel-framed building. Sadly the glass and terracotta brick cladding of the building has long been obscured by steel sheeting. The building is still in industrial use.

By the 1920s, building in stone for purposes other than ornamental feature or as a facing material was becoming prohibitively expensive. A stylistic rejection of Victorian extravagance had taken place alongside this, and was married to the widespread availability of new materials – stainless steel, toughened glass and plastics – producing the Art Deco style factory, unmistakably and unashamedly 'Brave New World'. There are few better examples than the Co-operative Luma light bulb factory in Shieldhall. Not an airport building, despite the bold frontal conning tower feature, but the SCWS showing off the skills of its in-house architect in the late 1930s. As a light bulb factory, light is the theme of the building, with its abundance of glass and stainless steel. Closed like all of the former SCWS factories at Shieldhall, the Luma has been converted to flats, and makes a fine landmark on the way to Glasgow airport.

Another excellent example of Art Deco industrial style can be found at the *Express* building in Glasgow's city centre. This is erroneously known today as the *Herald* building due to a later newspaper's occupancy, but it was the location of *The Scottish Daily Express* until 1974, when an occupation by the workers failed to prevent closure and centralisation of the newspaper's printing operations. The building was constructed in 1936 for Beaverbrook Newspapers by Owen Williams, who had also built the more famous Boots factory at Beeston. Though framed with re-enforced concrete, Williams covered the building in black vitrolite to eye-catching effect. After newspaper production finally ceased there, this building too became luxury flats.

In the 1950s a handful of quality industrial buildings were still being erected in Glasgow, such as the Wills Tobacco factory in Dennistoun, designed in-house by the firm's team of architects. With its grand entrance tower, designed in brick with concrete dressings, this is a late addition to our File. The building in Alexandra Parade was actually designed in the late 1930s, in an understated Art Deco style, but not constructed until after World War Two. Closed in the 1980s, it is now a successful business centre which employs as many as did the cigarette works, although of course with the much better working conditions of the 21st century.

In the last half-century few, if any, Fabulous Factories have been erected, either in Glasgow or elsewhere. Part of the reason is that the 1950s and 1960s saw the growth of peripheral industrial estates, where the ultra-utilitarian design of the factory made it largely indistinguishable from any other large building. On top of this, from the 1980s onwards, de-industrialisation meant that few factories were being built at all. Non-domestic architectural flair is now devoted to office blocks and shopping complexes, or to sports and cultural facilities, rather than to industrial buildings. Sadly, many old factory buildings, their architectural and aesthetic merit often hidden by misuse and decay, have been wantonly demolished without thought for potential redevelopment. Let us therefore enjoy, cherish, preserve against destruction, and strive for the re-use in some form of the remaining fabulous factories that the industrial era has left us. They are as important – I would dare say even more important – than all the stately homes that get so much attention from heritage conservationists and visitors to the area.

NOTE: as the distance from the Alexandria Argyll Works to New Lanark is in the region of over 50 miles, it is beyond the capabilities of all but fanatical urban explorers dedicated to taking a few days to do so to walk between them.

For less dedicated walkers the following might be helpful:

NEW LANARK is approachable from Lanark station. For opening times and other information regarding this UNESCO World Heritage Site, see www.newlanark.org.

WEIR'S CATHCART WORKS is out on its own just a short walk from Cathcart station.

The ARGYLL MOTOR WORKS is five minutes' walk from Alexandria station.

The offices of the NORTH BRITISH LOCOMOTIVE COMPANY are a short walk south from Springburn station.

Factory Walk

The following is suggested for an interesting amble from High Street Station on the east side of Glasgow's city centre, and is a walk that combines several of the buildings featured in this chapter.

DUKE STREET COTTON MILL can be approached, along its eponymous street, by a short walk eastwards from High Street station, and thence a ten minute stroll takes you down Barrrack Street and along the Gallowgate to the former CITY ABBATOIR. Heading down Abercromby Street and then taking a right turn brings the pedestrian to TEMPLETON'S CARPET FACTORY. Another five minutes along London Road and then up Bain Street brings the BARROWLAND CLAY PIPE FACTORIES into view and after that it is ten minutes back along the Gallowgate to High Street and its station. Before getting back on a train, a short walk to the west of the station along Ingram Street and then into Albion Street will take you to the former DAILY EXPRESS (HERALD) building in the heart of Merchant City cappuccino country. This walk takes you from the First World of the Merchant City to the Third World of Calton in little more than a square mile.

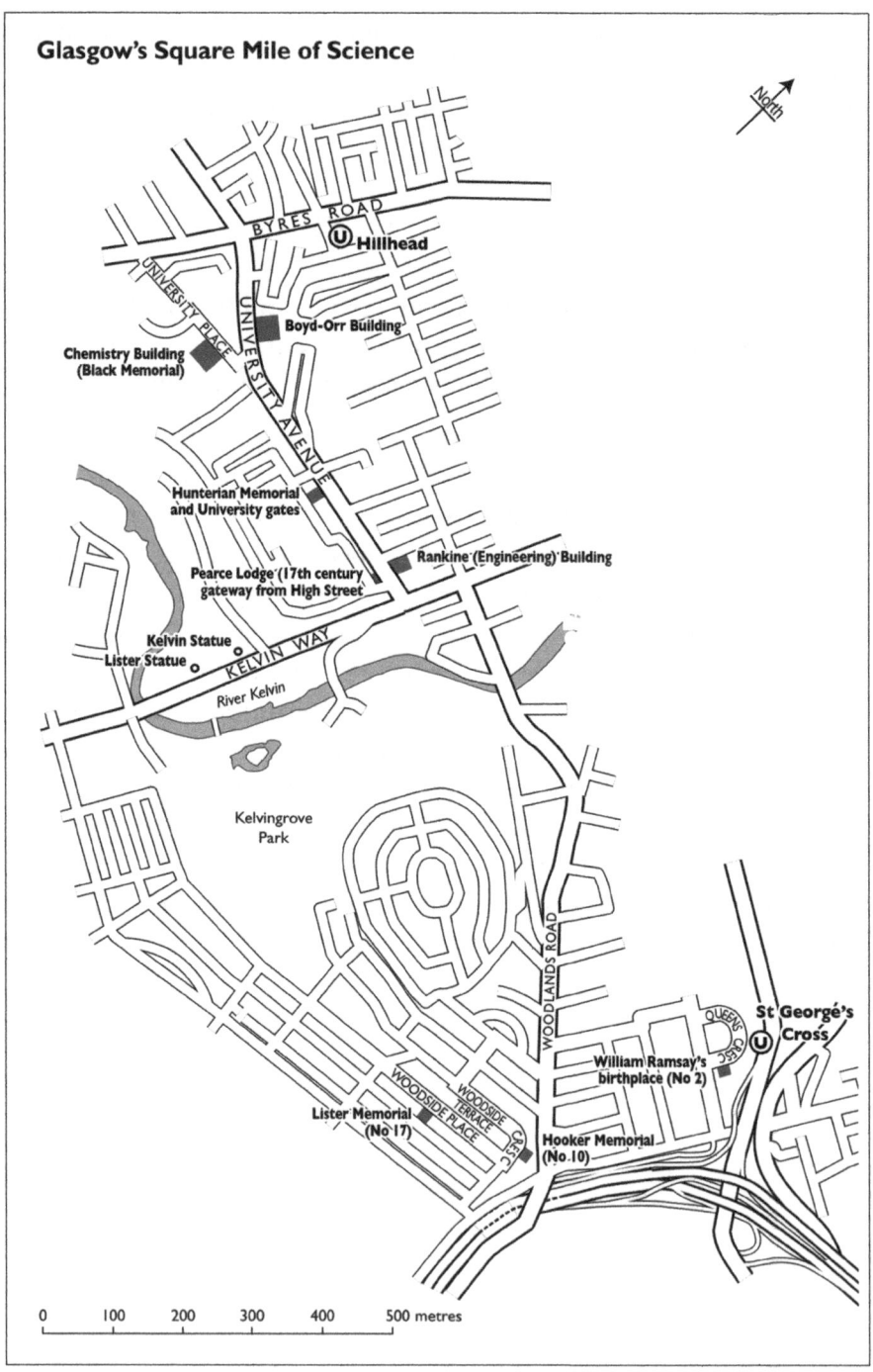

CHAPTER THREE

Glasgow's Square Mile of Science

MANY READERS WILL be familiar with the book by Jack House, *Square Mile of Murder*, which recounts the lust and lucre-motivated nefarious goings-on amongst some of the middle class denizens of Glasgow's West End in the later 19th and early 20th centuries. But there was more than murder and mayhem occurring in the grand terraces of the bourgeoisie at that time, and one could just as easily write a book on the area entitled *Square Mile of Science*, outlining the city's contribution to scientific development. This is beyond the scope of the present chapter, which will instead take the reader on a tour of some of the sites in the area associated with scientific achievement in the hope that he or she may be persuaded to undertake a ramble in what was, until World War One, Glasgow's most salubrious quarter at a period when the city had a real claim to the name 'Second City of Science'.

Starting at Hillhead subway station, a southwards walk down Byres Road takes you to University Avenue, where the first object to meet – perhaps even offend! – the eye is a tall concrete-clad building in the now unpopular architectural style of the early 1970s. This was named after John Boyd-Orr, who was born in 1880 in Ayrshire, graduated BSC from Glasgow University in 1910, and then worked in the University's Physiology Department before moving to the Rowatt Institute, outside Aberdeen, in 1923. There he studied animal and human nutrition, and helped lay the basis of government policies during World War Two and afterwards. A generation bred on cod liver oil and orange juice owes much of their good health to Boyd-Orr. Such was his international reputation that he was appointed the first Director of the UN Food and Agricultural Organisation from 1945–1948. He resigned from this post when he discovered that its activities were not to be concerned primarily with relieving hunger but with using food aid as an arm of US foreign policy in the looming Cold War. He was also an early supporter of nuclear disarmament, and a founding member of the Campaign for Nuclear Disarmament. Awarded the Nobel Peace Prize in 1949, he was Rector (1945) and Chancellor (1946) of Glasgow University, and died in 1971.

Rather more pleasing on the eye than the Boyd-Orr Building is the Institute of Chemistry across the road on University Place, a 'Roman' brick construction from the later 1930s. On the wall is a large plaque commemorating Joseph Black. Born in Bordeaux in 1728, Black studied at Glasgow University under William Cullen, and later at Edinburgh. His MD, described in the *Oxford Dictionary of National Biography* as the most original graduation thesis every written, was the first scientific identification of a gas distinct from air, that of carbon dioxide, which Black called 'fixed air'. He heated magnesium carbonate and collected the CO_2 released, quantifying and correctly analysing his results. He was appointed to the Chemistry Chair at Glasgow in 1756 where he completed his most important work, the discovery of both 'latent' and 'specific' heat, i.e. the amount of heat required to turn a body from a solid to liquid or liquid to gaseous state at the same temperature. It is only a slight exaggeration to say, as do Clement and Robertson in *Scotland's Scientific Heritage* (1961), that 'From these three major discoveries made within the space of six years... sprang the thermodynamics of the 19th century and the Industrial Revolution'.

Black had a lucrative industrial consultancy, advising on chemical and textile production to local entrepreneurs, and he also helped James Watt's research on the steam engine with scientific advice and an advance of £1,000. An inspiring teacher, hundreds attended his lectures and he formed the first Chemical Society in the world. He later moved to Edinburgh University, but undertook no further important work there. Black is often described as the 'father of modern scientific chemistry'.

A little uphill along University Avenue we come to the wrought-iron Memorial Gates, placed here in 1951, on the 500th anniversary of the University's foundation. It is astonishing that Joseph Black is not thereon commemorated, given his place in scientific history, but this mirrors a general neglect of Black, for, almost alone amongst great scientists of the later 18th century, he still awaits his biographer. Amongst the many luminaries from all disciplines honoured on the gates, however, is William Cullen, Black's university teacher. Born in Hamilton, he matriculated at Glasgow in 1726. He taught chemistry at Glasgow from 1744-1751 (after persuading the University to set up the Chair by a personal donation of £52!) then took over the Chair of Medicine at the University. In 1756 Cullen moved to the then-more-prestigious Edinburgh medical chair. A classifier rather than a man of original discoveries, Cullen no longer holds the esteemed reputation he had in his lifetime, though his *Materia Medica* of 1776 is regarded as the leading pharmacopoeia of its day.

A few steps inside the Memorial Gates and we arrive at the Hunterian Memorial of 1925, designed by JJ Burnet and with bronze reliefs by GH Paulin. The Hunter brothers William (b.1718) and John (b.1728) were Britain's most eminent medical practitioners in the 18th century. William left Glasgow University (where he studied with Cullen) in 1736 without a degree, though he was awarded a MD by the University in 1750. As a result of his *Anatomical Description of the Human Gravid Uterus* (1774), he is regarded as the founder of gynaecology. He developed a high-class London practise (counting Royalty among his patients) which made him very rich. On his death he left £5,000 to Glasgow University to build a museum for his collections. The Hunterian Museum is now one of the University's star attractions, and lies in the main building behind the memorial. His brother John did not attend any university, but nevertheless developed as a highly skilled surgeon in London, where he endowed another Hunterian Museum.

We drop downhill to the Pearce Lodge at the foot of University Avenue, and here encounter a charming 17th-century gatehouse, re-assembled from the High Street whence the University moved to its present location on Gilmorehill in the 1870s. The gatehouse is named after William Pearce, the Govan shipbuilder who funded the removal of the gatehouse from its High Street location to its present location. Through this gateway (though then located elsewhere) walked those we have already discussed – Black, Cullen and Hunter – as well as did Colin MacLaurin. He was born at Glendaruel, Argyll in 1698, son of a Kirk of Scotland minister, and graduated MA from Glasgow at the age of 16 with a thesis in defence of Newton's ideas of Universal Gravitation. By 19 he was Professor of Mathematics at Aberdeen University, later moving to the corresponding post in Edinburgh. He was a friend of Newton and a lifelong defender of his ideas, for instance in his *Treatise on Fluxions* (1742). He was also an original mathematician and Maclaurin's Theorem of mathematical analysis is still taught today. MacLaurin was a staunch Hanoverian. He died of pneumonia in 1746 after organising Edinburgh's defences against the Jacobites and then fleeing to England, though he did at least have the comfort of hearing of the defeat of the Pretender at Culloden shortly before his death.

Behind Pearce Lodge is the James Watt building. A native of Greenock, Watt worked at Glasgow University as a technician but had an extensive grasp of academic science in his own right. His steam engine research, which launched the industrialisation of the globe, was based on solid science and he also did other scientific work, being the first person to discover the chemical composition

The Old College (Swan's Views of Glasgow)
The University at its original medieval location on the High Street. It was here that Cullen and Black – and later Kelvin – studied, and where James Watt worked.

of water, though not the first to publish on the topic; it was Henry Cavendish who was to receive this credit. Fittingly, there are probably more statues of James Watt in Glasgow than anyone else; I personally know of six, the most famous being Chantrey's in George Square.

Just opposite the Pearce Lodge on University Avenue is the Rankine Building, another rather uninspired construction from the later 1960s. In keeping with the practical bent in its scientific endeavours, Glasgow University established the world's first Chair of Engineering in 1840, and the building is named after its second incumbent, William John Macquorn Rankine. He was born in Edinburgh, and worked as an industrial engineer before coming to Glasgow. He continued this technological focus once an academic, consulting, for example, on the provision of the city's water supply from Loch Katrine, designing 'Tennants Stalk', the huge chimney which disperse noxious fumes from the chemical factory at St Rollox, and working on the problem of metal fatigue in railways. He was recognised by being created the first President of the Institute of Engineers in Scotland. His main theoretical work was on fluid dynamics, out of which he developed his textbook *Shipbuilding, Theoretical and Practical* (1866), and more especially on thermodynamics, quantifying the convertibility of heat and work. He wrote the *Manual of the Steam Engine* (1859) and later elaborated the 'Rankine Cycle' to describe its workings. Rankine worked with his friend Kelvin on the laws of thermodynamics and some feel he should have greater recognition in this work than he has been awarded. He died in 1872, aged 52.

If we turn right down Kelvin Way after a few hundred yards we come to a delightful part of Kelvingrove Park, where the University tower looms over us. Here we encounter a fine pair of bronze public sculptures, the first a 1913 statue of Lord Kelvin (William Thomson, 1st Baron Kelvin). Born in 1824 in Belfast, Thomson moved to Glasgow in 1832 when his father (a Glasgow man himself) was awarded the Mathematics Chair at the University. Educated at home by his father and then at Cambridge University, Thomson was appointed to the Natural Philosophy (Physics) chair at Glasgow in 1846, a post he held for 53 years. Like many scientists he did his best work when still relatively young, being involved in the elaboration of the fundamental laws of thermodynamics in the early 1850s. The absolute scale of temperature is named after Kelvin. He was offered the Cavendish chair of Physics at Cambridge in 1871 but refused it in order to stay in Glasgow, a city he loved and where he was a convivial figure. Later, Kelvin's involvement in industrial consultancy and his economic activities (he held 70 patents at his death) overshadowed his scientific work. His compass was adopted by the Admiralty in 1889, before which he was the brains behind laying the first successful transatlantic cable in 1866. Ennobled as Lord Kelvin, he died with a fortune which today would be equivalent to £10 million. Regarded by the Victorians as the epitome of the successful scientist, Kelvin is buried beside Newton in Westminster Abbey.

Though Kelvin set up teaching laboratories at the new Gilmorehill campus and trained many competent practical scientists, he established no research laboratories or programmes after the fashion then becoming standard at Cambridge and University College London. His 50 year tenureship definitely stultified the Natural Philosophy Department in Glasgow – he was followed in the chair by no successor of note. In 1850 Glasgow was at the head of research in physics in the UK; in 1900 it was lagging behind UCL, Cambridge and Oxford. Kelvin was to an extent responsible for this. In certain areas his theoretical conservatism is open to criticism; despite his own work in electro-magnetism in the 1840s, Kelvin opposed Maxwell's electro-magnetic theory of light, and later opposed the new physics based on x-rays ('they will prove to be a hoax', he stated) and sub-atomic particles emerging at the end of the 19th century. However, it would be unreasonable to expect a man of around 75 to be able to keep up with what were extremely difficult and abstract new developments in physics.

Kelvin was a devout Christian and opposed developments which he saw as undermining religion – *but he opposed them scientifically*. He combated the geologists' uniformitarianism, according to which the physical world was the result of millennia of slow development, and behind which he saw evolutionary Darwinian anti-Christian ideas lurking. However, instead of quoting the Bible as many others did, on the basis of the physics of the day Kelvin demonstrated that 'provided no new source of energy was discovered', the Universe was simply not old enough for the timescale of geological uniformitarianism and biological evolution to have taken place. Indeed, at that time it was thought that the sun was a molten ball cooling down, and calculations of its age made from that premise; now we know it is basically a self-regenerating nuclear power station, and our revised estimates find it to be much older. He also pointed out – as did others – that Darwin proposed no real mechanism for evolution (Charles really should have opened the book on his genetic work that Mendel sent him!). Darwinism was on a shaky peg till at least the 1920s when knowledge of genetics – and the fact that the Universe was shown to be much older than had been thought – finally gave it the upper hand over its scientific and religious adversaries.

Though he was to be later proved wrong on evolution, Kelvin was undoubtedly right at the time to regard Darwinism as an unproven hypothesis, not just the old reactionary duffer as he is often portrayed. The real tragedy of Kelvin is not that he opposed ideas later proven to be correct, but that he was lured from his theoretical physical research into the lucrative and prestigious world of practical science with its glamour and wealth. Today it is James Clerk Maxwell – 'the man who changed everything' according to Einstein, who invented nothing but whose electro-magnetic theories of light laid the basis for wireless, television and radar – whom we regard as Scotland's greatest 19th-century scientist, rather than Kelvin – as did most of his contemporaries. Unlike with Black, Kelvin has an excellent biographer in David Lindley's *Degrees Kelvin: The Genius and Tragedy of William Thomson* (2004).

In the 18th century several Glasgow scientists (Cullen, Black, and MacLaurin) took part in a brain

KELVIN IN 1897.
When he finally retired, Kelvin became a bit of a celebrity globe trotter. Here is a cartoon from his North America trip in that year.

drain to the more prestigious Edinburgh University. In the 19th century, however, Glasgow's increasing reputation not only meant that it generally held onto home-grown men like Kelvin, but also attracted practitioners of science from elsewhere; Rankine, as noted, was from Edinburgh. A good example of reverse brain drain at that period was Joseph Lister, whose memorial stands a little downhill from Kelvin's. Paulin's 1923 statue of Lister (b.1827) commemorates his time as Professor of Surgery at Glasgow from 1860–1869, when the University was still on the High Street and the attached hospital was the Royal Infirmary, where Lister performed his famous experiments on antisepsis. Reading Pasteur in 1865 convinced Lister that infection came from miasma in the air, and he developed carbolic acid sprays as an antidote. Later it was established that infection came from many more areas than the air (such as the poor personal hygiene in medical personnel, which was apparently a notorious failing of Lister's), and others working at the time had as good results as Lister in patient survival, but Lister retains the fame. Crossing Kelvin Way, a walk through the delightful Kelvingrove Park takes you to Woodside Place, where at No. 17 there is a plaque on the wall commemorating Lister's residence in Glasgow, on a house where he reputedly gave the most frugal and dull dinner parties. Glasgow was, however, a stepping stone for the ambitious Lister, who later moved to London.

Now we are in the heart of 19th-century bourgeois Glasgow, in the Park District which housed the captains of industry, academics and clergymen of the city's elite in fine Victorian terraced houses, set back from private gardens, far from the squalid and overcrowded East End. The Park District is possibly the finest piece of Victorian town planning in the UK, but sadly at the end of Woodside Place, as we come to Woodside Terrace, a modern office block sits where Nos 1–5 Woodside Crescent used to be. However, No.10 still stands, and here we come to the Hooker residence. A plaque on the wall commemorates William Jackson Hooker, who was appointed Professor of Botany at Glasgow University in 1820, aged 35, again showing that Glasgow University had become if not a resting place then at least a respectable stepping stone for English scientists. A rich, enthusiastic amateur who had 'never lectured nor attended a lecture', he transformed the Botany Department, increasing student numbers and the size of its collection. Though it was not opened until the year after he moved back south to become the first full-time director at Kew Gardens, Hooker was responsible for the development of the Botanic Gardens on Great Western Road. He also wrote *Flora Scotica* (1821). Surprisingly the memorial at No 10 does not mention Hooker's at least equally famous son.

Born in Suffolk in 1817, John Dalton Hooker moved to Glasgow at the age of three, and attended Glasgow High School, before graduating MD from Glasgow University in 1839. He subsequently took part in an Arctic voyage in the *Erebus* on which he wrote *Flora Antarctica* (c.1844–47), followed by another journey to Sikkim which resulted in *Rhododendrons of the Sikkim Himalaya* (1849–1851). Hooker's research gave evidence for the theory of natural selection, and he was the first person in whom Charles Darwin confided his ideas on evolution and one of the first to champion those ideas in public. Like Darwin, he felt evolution undermined creationist ideas and was a religious sceptic, though also like Darwin he did not make this too public. On his father's death in 1865, JD Hooker was appointed director at Kew. Although he is not commemorated at the house in Woodside Crescent, the profusion of rhododendrons in the private gardens of Park acts as a memorial to him.

Moving on, we arrive at the pillared porticoes of the mansions of Woodside Terrace, where at No.3 William MacEwan lived till his death in 1924. Born in Bute in 1840, MacEwan was Britain's greatest surgeon in the 19th century, as the Hunters had been in the 18th. He studied under Lister at the Glasgow Royal Infirmary and later became Regius Professor of Surgery at Glasgow; in 1889 MacEwan turned down a move to John Hopkins University in the USA, again showing that Glasgow was able in the 19th century to hold, attract, and often retain top-flight scientific and medical practitioners. MacEwan carried out the first brain tumour removal and the first open-chest operations, proving that this did not cause the lungs to collapse, as well as pioneering bone transplant surgery. A genuinely humane man, MacEwan also gave willingly of his time in developing prosthetic limbs for servicemen mutilated by the Great War.

By MacEwan's death in 1924, Glasgow's economy was in decline and so too was the Park District as rich people moved to the suburbs and town houses were converted to offices, hotels and sometimes more dubious usages. In the last 20 years this process has been reversed and more town house are being converted into up-market flats. On the next stage of our walk, however, this has not yet happened, and the area has a demotic rather than a bourgeois air to it. Half way along Woodside Terrace a right turn takes you to Lynedoch Street where you drop down, cross Woodlands Road and follow Ashley Street to West Princes Street. On the right across the road is Queen's Crescent, one of Glasgow's most prestigious addresses when it was built in the 1840s. The street is now sadly dilapidated, with some houses lying derelict, though surprisingly the private gardens are still in good condition. Here at No.2 was the birthplace of one who many might regard as Glasgow's greatest scientist since Joseph Black.

William Ramsay was born in 1852 into a scientific-engineering family background, and graduated from Glasgow University before doing his PhD (then a one year degree) in Germany in 1872. Germany was the world's frontrunner in chemistry at this time. Ramsay taught chemistry at Glasgow till 1879, then moved to Bristol and finally to become Chair of Chemistry at University College London in 1887. He established a research programme at UCL to fill one of the gaps in Mendeleev's Periodic Table of the elements, discovering in the process the so-called inert gases of argon, helium, krypton and xenon. For this he was awarded the Nobel Prize in Chemistry in 1904. Ramsay is commemorated with a bronze plaque outside the Bute Hall in the main University building on Gilmorehill.

Unlike many scientists, Ramsay continued well into his middle age to be at the forefront of research in the increasingly blurred field between physics and chemistry, studying the recently discovered phenomena associated with radioactive decay. With Frederick

Soddy at UCL, Ramsay showed that radon decay produced helium nuclei, the first experimental verification of the transmutation of elements. The philosopher's stone of the alchemists had, after centuries of being equated with all that was unscientific, finally been shown to exist. Soddy himself later moved to the Chemistry Department at Glasgow and there in 1912 demonstrated the existence of radioactive isotopes, for which he was awarded the Nobel Prize in 1921 – though by that time he had moved to Oxford. A recent proposal to dispose of 'Soddy's Box', in which he kept his radioactive samples, was dropped due to public outcry and the materials are now likely to find a suitable home in the Hunterian Museum.

Another great scientist associated with the Chemistry Department at Glasgow was Alexander Todd, who was born in the city, the son of a railway worker, in 1907. After education at Glasgow University, he became Professor of Chemistry at Cambridge and was awarded the Nobel Prize in 1957 for his work on the structures of large organic molecules. Though not commemorated at Gilmorehill, he is memorialised in the form of the University's suburban Todd Campus which stands next the Kelvin Campus.

We end our square mile of science in Queen's Crescent, ironically close to where Jack House ended his square mile of murder stories with the grizzly tale of Marion Gilchrist's demise in West Princes Street, the crime for which Oscar Slater was framed. Hopefully Queen's Crescent will undergo restoration before it is too late, and we may one day see a memorial to Ramsay at his birthplace. The Subway led us to the start of our trail; a few steps from Queen's Crescent, St George's Cross station allows the Subway to bring it to an end. Glasgow has many virtues, but one that is not self-serving is an excessive modesty. As in many other areas, the contribution of the city to the world's corpus of scientific knowledge has been massively disproportionate to its size, and we should do more to celebrate this. The recently inaugurated annual Science Festival under the aegis of Glasgow and Strathclyde Universities is a welcome step in the right direction. And the hugely successful West End Festival now offers a Science Walk through the University and Park districts, based on the materials highlighted in this chapter.

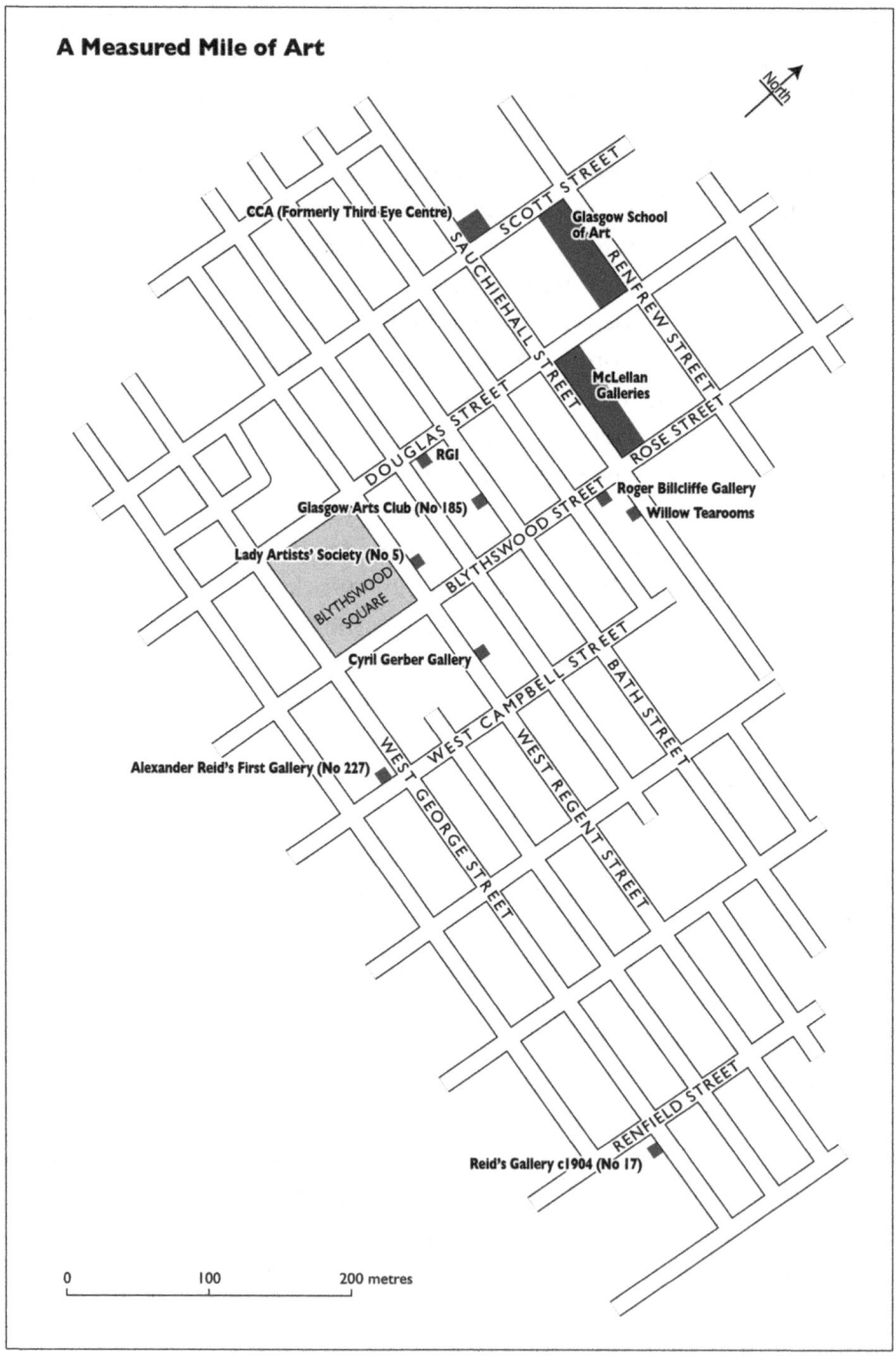

CHAPTER FOUR

A Measured Mile of Art

GLASGOW'S ARTISTIC LIFE did not develop at a raging creative gallop, but was rather an intermittent process. There was a brief moment of glory with the creation of the Foulis brothers' Academy of the Fine Arts in the 18th century, but this largely petered out, with the development of a successful art scene still a century away. It left us, however, a fascinating 1761 depiction by David Allan of the *Foulis Academy Exhibition, Inner Court of the Old College of Old Masters*. The city briefly became a minor art centre in the early 19th century, with local painters (notably John Knox and later his pupil Horatio MacCulloch) based there. Knox combined landscape paintings of places like the Trossachs, Arran and Loch Lomond with scenes of urban life in Glasgow such as *Old Glasgow Bridge* and *Old Glasgow Cross*. These, along with productions like Swann's *Select Views of Glasgow* (1828) showed that the urban middle class took an interest and pride in their own city at that time. However, with increasing urbanisation, population growth and urban squalor in Glasgow, as in other Victorian cities, tastes were subject to radical and intense change.

MacCulloch made his name as one of the most famous Victorian landscape artists in Scotland during the 19th century. He eschewed urban scenes altogether for dramatic and romantic depictions of the Western Highlands, his sights ranging from Skye to Argyll, as rural escapist painting – exemplified, for example, by *My Heart's in the Highlands* – became one of the dominant genres in mid-Victorian art. Edinburgh, however, with its artistic identity firmly established by The Royal Scottish Academy and National Galleries of Scotland, dominated the art scene in Scotland till the later decades of the 19th century. This was reflected by MacCulloch's move to the capital, undertaken as his fame blossomed and peaked in the 1850s and 1860s with works like *The Cuillin from Ord*. Later in the century, following a period of wealth and population drift, the centre of gravity for Scottish artistic creativity shifted towards

Glasgow, where, with brief intermissions, it has arguably remained since. A good example of this shift is that of Edinburgh-born artist JD Fergusson, who, after living for many years in France, returned to Scotland in 1939 to spend his last decades in Glasgow, which he regarded as the more creative of the two cities.

Then, as now, the centre of this artistic world was around Blythswood Hill, an area of former bourgeois townhouses dating from the early 19th century. By its later decades, these homes had been largely abandoned for fresher fields further west, and they thereafter provided excellent accommodation not only for offices, but also for clubs, galleries and artists' studios. With this chapter, let us go walkabout in this *quartier* and enjoy the gallery and café culture which it boasts today. It is an easy mile of an amble, all told, what we might call a 'measured mile of art'.

Alexander Reid had led an exciting life in bohemian Paris in the 1880s, including sharing a flat with Vincent Van Gogh (who painted the portrait of Reid now hanging in Kelvingrove Art Gallery). Most intriguing is that he almost shared a suicide pact with the artist as well. Such radical actions set aside, he returned to Glasgow and set up as an art dealer with his *Société des Beaux Arts* gallery in 1889. Life was to be less exciting than in Paris, but also more lucrative as he gradually became Scotland's leading art dealer and one of the foremost in Britain. Indeed, much of the world famous and highly celebrated Burrell Collection was amassed by Reid. The art dealer has become the subject of a major and fascinating biography by Frances Fowle, *Van Goch's Twin* (2010)

At the bottom of Blythswood Hill at 117 West George Street was the gallery Reid ran in around 1904, and it is a convenient starting point for our tour. The gallery was housed over two floors in the then recently constructed Sun Life Insurance Building, designed by the architect William Leiper (who had previously constructed the famous Templeton's carpet factory on Glasgow Green). The block was built in the *Beaux Arts* style and the French liked the building so much that it gained a Silver Medal in the Paris Exhibition of 1900. The former insurance office in the building, now *Sarti's* restaurant, forms a sumptuous marble sculpture palace in which to enjoy a fortifying coffee before proceeding. Kaffe and Kultur gang thegither.

This was not Alexander Reid's first gallery; to see where that lay we must walk steeply up West George Street, climbing Blythswood Hill, and passing Ewan Mundy Fine Art, to reach No. 227 (on the corner with West Campbell Street). This building was designed in the dominant neo-classical style of the bourgeois townhouses which mushroomed here along grid-plan lines in the 1820s and 1830s. It was at No. 227 that Reid began to introduce the Glasgow public to new developments in French and European art, to Impressionism and Post-Impressionism, long before they became fashionable in Edinburgh or even in London. That not all were taken with Reid's efforts to educate the Glasgow public is evinced by Catherine Carswell's comments in her autobiography, *Lying Awake*. When she attended, and was herself impressed by these radical works, she mused how,

> uncultured and uninformed, I stood alone among the jeering and sniggering crowd at the first exhibition in Scotland of the French impressionists. Here was something that was all mine…

It was also in the West George Street gallery that Reid promoted the emerging artistic school later known as the Glasgow Boys; painters such as James Guthrie, John Lavery and Joseph Crawhall, all influenced by the new trends in French art, who collectively were the most important painters in Britain in the 1880s and 1890s. Possibly less sure of their own taste, and relying on that of Reid, the new money of the Glasgow industrial and commercial bourgeoisie was more willing to buy these artists than the older wealth represented by Edinburgh. They had more of that wealth to dispose of, moreover, for the riches of Glasgow and the West of Scotland in this period almost defy belief. James Baird of Gartsherrie and Charles Tennant of St Rollox, for example, were two of the richest ten men in Europe, and others such as the Coats of Paisley were not far behind.

Like their French counterparts, the Glasgow Boys painted mainly country themes, but unlike their predecessors such as MacCulloch –

painters they described as 'glue pots' – they painted Lowland rural life in a realistic manner, rather than Highland life in a romanticised one. A particularly treasured area with the Boys, not to mention their imitators and successors, was the countryside around Kirkcudbright, a town which became an artists' colony of sorts. In *To Pastures New* and *Old Willie*, James Guthrie depicted rural people with realism and only a trace of sentimentality, as did George Henry in *Noon* or *The Hedgecutter*. On occasion, the one or other of the School did approach urban reality, such as in William Kennedy's fine work of 1887, *Stirling Station*, but the one thing the Glasgow Boys never painted was Glasgow! Indeed, at the height of its wealth, but also at the height of its squalor and griminess, the city was not seen as an object worthy of artistic contemplation. John Lavery painted scenes of civic dignitaries at public events, such as *Glasgow Exhibition 1888*, and of the suburban middle-class playing tennis in *A Rally*, but these are scenes in the city, not of the city. The still-rising status of 'the Boys' is demonstrated by the fact that an entire room at Kelvingrove Art Gallery is now devoted to a permanent exhibition of the city's collection of their work, as their reputation – and the prices paid for their works – continues to grow year by year.

Although it is undeniable that in the High Victorian period the art-buying public wanted in the main to hang the countryside on its walls, there remained a market in Glasgow for urban scenes in the tradition established by Swann, exemplified in the very popular paintings of William 'Crimea' Simpson and David Small. Whilst Simpson's *Forty Glasgow Drawings* and Small's watercolours were guilty of depicting 'Auld Lang Syne' views of Glasgow in its past or quaint relics, both these artists painted some industrial scenes of life on the River Clyde, showing shipyards and commercial traffic. Simpson even depicted Dixon's *Govan Ironworks*, but these were exceptions rather than a rule for the interests of their artistic contemporaries.

West George Street leads us up to the crown of Blythswood Hill and to Blythswood Square, a development of splendid townhouses set around a formerly private garden. In the mid-to-late 19th century, this was the most prestigious address in Glasgow. The days when a Glasgow dealer was the main conduit of European art into Britain, as Reid was, will probably never return, but Glasgow still has several galleries on Blythswood Hill where enterprising dealers continue to host exhibitions and showcase the best of contemporary Scottish and British art. One of these is just off Blythswood Square, a little downhill in West Regent Street, where we find the current establishment of a stalwart of the Glasgow art scene for over 60 years, Cyril Gerber's Fine Art Gallery. Recently deceased, Cyril Gerber was a central figure in the post-war Glasgow art world, and the current gallery bearing his name was preceded by others such as the Compass Gallery in 1969 and, before that, the New Charing Cross Gallery, which gave space to the works of artists like Bett Low, Joan Eardley and John Taylor.

A little downhill and around the corner in Blythswood Street sits another gallery that merits mention; the Roger Billcliffe Gallery, which we shall investigate later. Both of these galleries were very active in the promotion of the New Glasgow Boys school of the 1980s which, a century after their namesakes had flourished, and after a fairly arid period for painting in the city in the 1960s and 1970s, had a profound effect on art in the UK and on re-establishing Glasgow as a City of Culture. Unlike the Glasgow Boys of the 1880s, who painted mainly rural scenes appealing to the escapist desires of their rich urban patrons, the New Boys such as Howson, Currie, Wiszniewski and Campbell were heavily influenced by urban imagery, especially that which reflected Glasgow's industrial past and then-current industrial decline. A fine quartet of paintings executed in 1995–96, one by each of these four artists, hangs in the foyer of the Glasgow Concert Hall at the foot of Sauchiehall Street, and is worth a visit after taking this tour. Wizniewski's is called *Concert Hall* and shows angelic musicians in that dreamlike whimsical context he favours, whilst Campbell's *Pillow of Dreams,* with its images of Mount Rushmore alongside the widow of John Smith and an onlooking industrial worker, appears to express a somewhat misplaced hope in the intentions of the Labour Party of that time. The most powerful images can be found in Howson's *My Great Heart,* a depiction of the brute violence produced by social marginalisation, painted with an intensity Howson has arguably lost since he started mass-producing religious imagery. Last is Currie's *Forest*, where a group of people stand like trees, blind and pale-faced. This painting appears to express Currie's disillusionment with social developments since his People's Palace murals from the 1980s (discussed in Chapter Five).

Back to Blythswood Square. At No. 5 is a house whose Art Nouveau exterior is at odds with the classical symmetry of the rest of the square. This is the Glasgow Society of Lady Artists, formed in 1882, which was to be a gathering place for the Glasgow Girls group of artists, including Margaret and Frances MacDonald and Bessie MacNicol. They were the female counterpart to the movement initiated by Charles Rennie Mackintosh in the 1880s. Mackintosh himself designed the remodelled stonework and doorway of No.5, as well as some of the interior for the Society of Lady Artists in 1908. Planning permission would never be granted for this today! An even more famous house stands next door at No.6, Madeleine Smith House, named after the one-time female occupant who was accused in a notorious mid-Victorian murder trial of killing her lover with poisoned chocolate.

The longest survivor on the Glasgow art scene, which recently celebrated its 150th birthday, is the Royal Glasgow Institute of the Fine Arts, which now lies just around the corner from Blythswood Square, on Douglas Street. Founded in 1861, the RGI offered a forum for new painting and younger Scottish artists, as well as exhibiting other British and Continental painters in its later years. Their annual exhibitions before the First World War were regarded as second in the UK only to those of the Royal Academy in London. Success made the RGI become part of the art establishment, and between the Great Wars of the 20th century it ceased to stand at the vanguard of new developments in painting, a situation which has been rectified in recent years.

Clubs constituted an important part of the art scene, in Glasgow none more so that the Glasgow Art Club, which can be reached by carrying on down Douglas Street to Bath Street, and taking a right turn past the Scotlandart Gallery. Originally founded in 1867, the Club acquired this pair of A-Listed 1830s town houses and the buildings were remodelled internally by the architects for whom Rennie Mackintosh worked. Mackintosh himself most probably had an influence on the restructuring. The Glasgow Art Club not only held exhibitions, but was a social gathering place holding dinners and balls. It still functions in this capacity today, with a bar and restaurant, and a venue which hosts concerts and other events. It has made a successful attempt to come out of a period of semi-hibernation and reach out to a wider public. Though less stuffy and conservative possibly than its Edinburgh counterparts, the Glasgow Art Club was not without its traditionalist limitations; several of the Glasgow Boys were initially refused membership when they applied, though later they were all to become members and have their work displayed at exhibitions.

As well as the clubs and galleries existing on Blythswood hill, many of the artists active in the city from the 1870s till about 1940 had their studios and living quarters here. Both Guthrie and Lavery had Bath Street addresses in the 1880s, and David Gauld, another Glasgow Boy, could be found in Blythswood Square in the 1900s. Leslie Hunter, the eminent Colourist, was based in West George Street in the 1920s. Though not Glasgow-born, he ended up in the city where he made a living painting portraits and rural themes, such as his wonderful *Houseboats, Balloch*. The Scottish Colourists were not so intimately connected with Glasgow as were the previous Glasgow Boys School, though both Hunter and JD Fergusson ended up in the city. But the west of Scotland still provided the main market for their works, having a more adventurous buying clientele, and, at that time, more money than the capital. Edinburgh-based JS Peploe, one of the pre-eminent Colourists, recognised this in 1911 when he wrote that he felt

> inclined to give up trying Edinburgh ever again… They want me to keep on doing the things I did ten years ago… How different those Glasgow people are from Edinburgh people. Plenty money.

The last main artist to have worked on Blythswood Hill appears to have been the sculptor Benno Schotz, who was still operating in

West Campbell Street in the 1930s. Those were hard times for artists as they sought work in the wake of the Crash of 1929, and Schotz recalls in his biography *Bronze in My Blood* that in one year of the 1930s his total sales of his work amounted to just £10! In this he was not alone. Sales at Reid's firm, which had been run since his death in 1928 by his son, were so poor that the *Société des Beaux Arts* closed its doors and re-located to London in 1932.

The Second World War, contrary to what one might expect, stimulated artistic life in Glasgow. As mentioned above, JD Fergusson came to live in the city in 1939. When he first returned, he lived at the recently built Beresford Hotel in Sauchiehall Street, just down from Blythswood Hill, before moving to the West End with his partner Margaret Morris. Her book *The Art of J.D. Fergusson* provides a fascinating perspective on the artistic life of the city during and after World War Two. Fergusson was inspired by Glasgow to paint, especially by the 'rural' aspects of Glasgow as depicted in his fine works such as *Spring in Glasgow, Red Dress, Botanic Gardens* and the *River Kelvin.* The city had none of the glowing, glamorous boulevards of Paris that had inspired a younger Fergusson, alas. Other artists, many of them Jewish, came as refugees to the city during the conflict, such as Joseph Hermann and Jankel Adler, who in turn influenced young local painters such as Bett Low and Joan Eardley. Hermann and Adler eventually moved on, although other refugees such as Hilda Goldwag remained in the city.

A left turn a little beyond the Glasgow Art Club on Bath Street down Blythswood Street takes us past the very attractive frontage of the Roger Billcliffe Gallery, mentioned earlier, to Sauchiehall Street, which forms the boundary between Blythswood hill to its south and Garnethill to the north. Here we are still very much in artistic territory. Artists needed places to eat and drink, and just around the corner from the Roger Billcliffe gallery are the famous Willow Tearooms, designed by Mackintosh for Miss Cranston in 1903–1904 and patronised by the artistic set of the Edwardian era. Even if not thirsty, it is worth taking a trip inside to wonder at the amazing interior whilst enjoying your tea and scones. Currently there is some doubt over the future of the Willow Tearooms, and the building is in need of extensive repair. Given the money Mackintosh brings into the city it would be criminal if funds were not found for restoration.

Passing westwards here, we see on the right the McLellan Galleries, a building indicative of the wealth produced by Victorian Glasgow in that it was built as the private gallery (with permitted public access) of coach builder and property developer Archibald McLellan. When he died in 1854 his collection became, with the building, the property of Glasgow Corporation and formed the nucleus of the city's art collection. The fact that almost all of McLellan's paintings consisted of Dutch and Italian Old Masters shows the taste of mid-nineteenth-century Glasgow, a taste that Alexander Reid did so much to inform and evolve. Incidentally, the Corporation paid £30,000 for the building and £15,000 for McLellan's paintings, which are now worth many hundred times those figures. The Galleries under Corporation ownership provided another location for exhibitions and art shows by such as the RGI and Reid's *Beaux Arts Society* until 1901, when its collection was moved to Kelvingrove Museum. At present a somewhat neglected facility, plans have been aired recently regarding bringing the McLellan galleries back into the mainstream of Glasgow's art scene. In the 1920s it was widely used by Reid and his *Société des Beaux Arts* to showcase modern French painting, as Reid moved from promoting the Impressionists to bringing the Post-Impressionists such as Gaugin and Cezanne to the attention of the Scottish art world.

An amble of a few 100 yards further west brings us to what might be seen as the 20th-century equivalent of the McLellan Galleries, now named the Centre for Contemporary Arts (CCA), but still known by Glaswegians of a certain age as the Third Eye Centre, under which name it originally opened as an arts venue. As well as refocusing its exhibitions on many of the artists who were active in Glasgow in the 1940s and 1950s (such as Bett Low and Joseph Herman), the Third Eye was an important place for the exhibition of the work of the New Glasgow Boys of the 1980s and 1990s. The gallery is itself situated in a masterpiece, Alexander 'Greek'

Thomson's Grecian Halls, built in 1865, though sadly little remains of the original interior to match the grand exterior.

Next, if you don't mind a steep patch uphill once again, you come to a building that few would dispute was an even greater masterpiece than Thomson's and which overlooks this whole artistic quarter of Glasgow. This is one of Glasgow's, Britain's and even the world's greatest architectural treasures, Charles Rennie Mackintosh's Glasgow School of Art, reached by climbing Douglas Street. It was not the revered institution it was to become until taken over by Fra Newberry in 1885, who began to transform everything from the teaching to the building itself, the present one constructed according to designs by Mackintosh from 1899 to 1909. Arguably the peer of any art school in the UK, the Glasgow School of Art has continued to produce a stream of talented artists. There were many raised eyebrows in London (and doubtless a few in Edinburgh) at the third consecutive award of the prestigious Turner Prize to a former student of Glasgow School of Art. This is not, however, the 'Glasgow Miracle' some talked about, but an expression of the fact that, for most of the last 150 years, Glasgow has often been at the forefront of artistic innovation.

For a city to flourish artistically at any period, several factors need to operate at once. There has to be an institution (or institutions) which function as an ideas powerhouse; there has to be a cluster of places where artists can meet, be it cafés, clubs, studios or galleries willing to exhibit their works; and, last but not least, there must exist an audience which provides patronage in the form of an art-buying public. The artist starving in his garret is not usually a productive one. These factors combine to produce what has been called an *artistic ecology*. Glasgow had all these a century or more ago, and, though in a different form, has them all today.

The image of Glasgow as a desert for the fine arts before about 1850 has been forcefully and successfully challenged in George Fairfull-Smith's *The Wealth of a City: the Fine Arts in Glasgow 1641–1830*, (2010) which came to my attention after my own book had been typeset.

CHAPTER FIVE

Artistic Representations of Labour in Glasgow

WILLIAM BELL SCOTT'S *Iron and Coal* (1861), painted for Wallington Hall in Northumberland, is probably the most famous visual image of labour we have from the Victorian era. The work depicts scenes from the heavy industries which were emerging at the time, and portrays the workers employed by them, complete with their tools and characteristic clothes. The image is widely used by social and art historians, arguably because it is the best of only a handful of examples of public art which utilised labour as their theme during Britain's period of industrialisation. By public art I refer to works of art, whether paintings, sculpture, stained glass or other artefacts, which were designed for, and are currently or were previously on display in, public spaces such as parks or streets, town halls or other public buildings such as banks or churches. This chapter does not discuss artworks hanging in public art galleries, or in private collections, which have been examined in greater detail elsewhere by any number of dedicated art historians.

It seems remarkable that during the century or more when machinery and manual labour combined to change the face of the United Kingdom, those two realities very rarely appeared as the subject of art at all, whether in private art produced for individual collectors, or in a more public forum. One of the main characteristics of manual labour in the period of industrialisation was its invisibility. In Scotland, as with the rest of Britain, the subject matter of 19th-century art ranged far and wide, from classical antiquity and to biblical times through to the medieval period, and up to contemporary scenes. However, the subject matter of contemporary art was far from representative of contemporary life. The more the peasantry declined as a social class, the more they appeared in art.

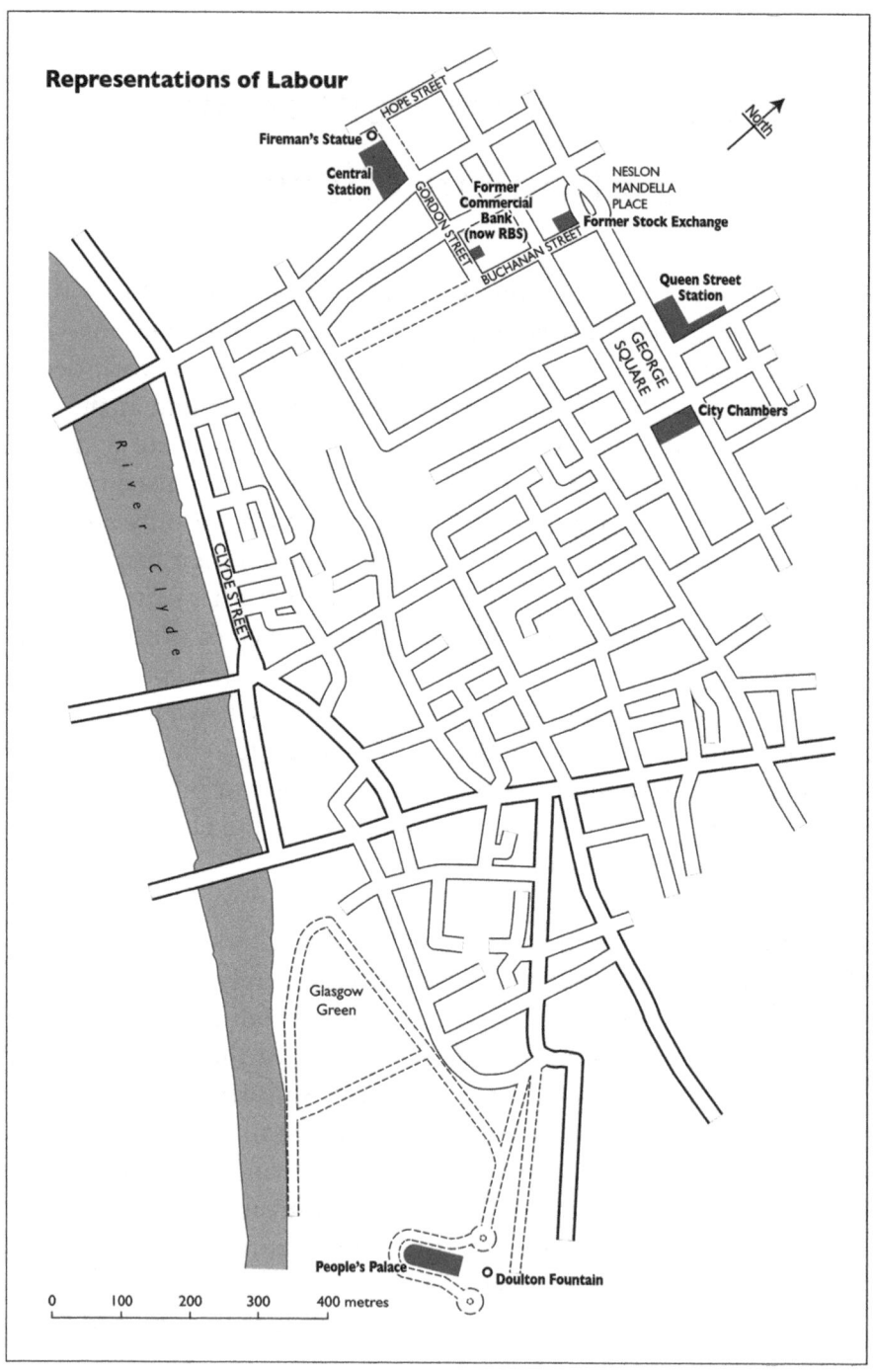

Images of the streetscapes of the bourgeois city and of the bourgeoisie themselves also accounted for a large proportion of the output of artists, with painters such as Lavery making a good living from portraiture of Victorian and Edwardian celebrities. The themes of art ranged globally, mirroring the capitalism which was conquering the globe, to absorb foreign lands and peoples. From the Orient to the Americas, exotic subjects found themselves depicted by brush and chisel, and artists such as Hornel, who took Japanese people and culture as his subject, built their fame on this exoticism.

In all this, labour was the theme that dared not speak its name. Though the Victorians and their successors were aware that industry and commerce had shaped their world, they acknowledged it only grudgingly in art. There is a certain irony in this, as it was the increased wealth produced by industrialisation that increased the market for art at that time beyond the previous elite of aristocratic buyers to the growing army of middle class purchasers. This in turn sustained a greater body of artistic workers, who ignored rather than bit the hand that indirectly fed them. Even where it appeared, labour tended to be sanitised, until its representation to the modern eye becomes almost comical. Often scenes of labour are re-cast in biblical or classical contexts, or their protagonists become idealised as virginal maidens, cherubic or angelic figures. As well as the dearth of depictions of contemporary personal clothing or tools, what is conspicuously absent in representations of public labour in art in the 19th century is power-driven machinery.

It might possibly be argued that this allegorical and historicist aspect to their art is a product of the Victorians seeing themselves as the inheritors of previous great European civilisations, and even as the guardians of contemporary non-European cultures, but if we look at artistic images, including those in public art, depicting war and the military in the 19th century and beyond, a different picture emerges. Here, despite the presence of religious and mythological iconography, the representation of the combatants is extremely lifelike. Military equipment, clothing, and the soldiers themselves are cast in a mode of heroic realism. The military are the only 'working men' whose activities are, in general, portrayed accurately at the height of the industrial era. Why a society should chose to largely ignore its industrial workers, or to transform them and their activity into something unrepresentative of the reality of 19th-century labour, whilst at the same time erecting predominantly realistic monuments to its soldiery (who comprised a tiny proportion of the population), it is not difficult to explain. The military was the vanguard of British imperialism and its conquest of the world, in which the upper and middle classes took great pride; they could thus be looked squarely in the face, without guilt or fear.

Classes Laborieuses, Classes Dangereuses (roughly 'the working class is a dangerous class') certainly provides part of the reason for the invisibility or lack of realism in the portrayal of industrial labour. Most artists were after all drawn out of the middle and upper classes, and would have shared the widespread contemporary fear of and distaste for the industrial masses. Guilt might also have played a part, it being unlikely that those seeking inspiration in Classical Antiquity or the Gothic Revival would have been happy admitting their bread was buttered by unlovely proletarians. However, simple ignorance was also surely a factor. The peasant was widely visible in the rural thematic context so beloved of Victorian painters, as too were fishermen in romantic coastal settings; as many canvases in Victorian times were devoted to depicting fishermen as to moving a fleet of sailing ships. So too, to an extent, were soldiers visible – in public displays or commemorations of military campaigns. Most people would have known what peasants, fishermen and soldiers looked like. Industrial labour, conducted behind factory walls or underground in mines, was largely invisible to those not directly involved, and unless they made the effort (and why should they?) most middle class people would simply never have seen such work being performed. Had there been a market for scenes of industrial production, artists would surely have obliged, but there was none. Individual proletarians were not art buyers and the labour movement, even when it later became powerful, rarely spent money on art – and at this time it was struggling even to exist. The middle-and upper-class buying public wanted art that reassured them, art that mirrored their view of the world, rather than images of the barbarian enemies at the gate.

Glasgow was the paradigmatic Victorian industrial city, and it shared in this mind-set which rendered contemporary labour largely invisible. The city has a collection of public sculptures second to none for a place of its size – which amounted to roughly a million people in the early 20th century. There also exists an unrivalled account of this particular art form in Ray McKenzie's *Sculpture in Glasgow* (1999), a book as gorgeously illustrated as it is informative. Art reflects social reality, though not always directly. If it did, the visitor would conclude from the sculptures on display that 19th-century Glasgow was a city of eminent bourgeois industrialists, clergy and politicians, with a smattering of poets and scientists. Overall, though, the impression given is a city of many, many military men. I direct you to McKenzie's book for a fuller study of these memorials.

Many of the larger pieces of sculpture in the city are military commemorations or celebrations of Empire. The Wellington Memorial in Exchange Square by Carlo Marochetti incorporates highly realistic casts of the Battle of Waterloo, while Lord Roberts' monument by Bates in Kelvingrove Park illustrates the multi-racial composition, from squaddy to sepoy, of the British Army on its march from Kandahar to Kabul (though not on its disastrous march back). The Doulton Fountain on Glasgow Green, the world's largest terracotta monument, shows the soldiers and the native inhabitants of the various parts of the British Empire in noble, although still lifelike, form – but not a single manual worker. The fine Cameronian War Memorial from 1924 by Philip Lindsey Clark, situated outside Kelvingrove Art Gallery, carried this tradition of military realism into the post-Great War period.

Whilst the Glasgow bourgeois could have comforted himself with these sculptures that affairs of Kirk and State were being looked after by great men, and the country and colonies were being defended by a heroic army, he would have looked hard and far before being reminded of how his own country earned its daily bread. Most architecture – even industrial buildings – when adorned with sculpture, avoided labour as a theme. The city abattoir and meat market feature a fine collection of sculpture, from the heads of various edible animals to the Greek god Pan, but there is not a slaughterman in sight. William Young's Glasgow City Chambers, completed in 1888, has splendid reliefs on its façade by John and William Mossman, the leading public sculptors in Glasgow in the 19th century. Amongst these are men at work, building ships, weaving and forging – but clad in classical togas and with sandals on their feet, and all using pre-industrial machinery.

The Mossman firm also executed the carvings on the Glasgow Stock Exchange of 1874, commemorating Art, Science, Industry and Commerce, all of which are represented by female figures. The relief on this Gothic Revival building representing *Engineering* is a medieval maiden holding a cogwheel. For *Building* and *Mining*, the mason and miner are both cast in medieval garb, and interestingly, whilst Mossman gets the mason's mallet correct (he would have seen his workmen use it all the time), he had clearly never been down a mine, as the sculpted miner carries an axe, not a pick. *Building* and *Mining* are two of the very few allegorical representations of labour in Glasgow that actually feature male workers.

Banks and insurance companies generally had money to throw at their new buildings, and again these can be revealing in their sculptural additions. In the former Commercial Bank on Gordon Street, a Royal Bank of Scotland premises from the 1850s onwards, those Victorians curious as to how coins and notes were manufactured would have been surprised to see on the building's frontage that not only were these produced in hand presses as they had been for centuries, but that the labour force in the Mint consisted of cherubs. However, when the bank's interior was remodelled in 1941, a set of 12 plaster plaques of Glasgow's industries by James H Clark was added. This set of works may not be of outstanding artistic merit, aiming as they do mainly at accurate representation, but they are probably one of the largest collections of art illustrating labour and industrial production on public display anywhere. The attitude they convey towards both the work process and the workers themselves is highly positive.

There are four landscapes and eight smaller medallion images. They depict a composite range of men and women at work in a highly realistic manner, including an engineer at his lathe, a female printing worker, bus workers and iron moulders, as well as two men working with a cement mixer. Clothes are accurately represented for the 1930s, with bunnets and dungarees being features of the men's working fashion. The miners are shown underground working with picks and shovels, as most coal mines were still un-mechanised, but the plaque representing Shipbuilding shows a crew working with a power-driven caulking gun, and that of the railway station features the latest in high speed trains, the *City of Glasgow*. The inclusion of an aviator with his aeroplane complements this fascination with speed and modernity. Unfortunately the bank now claims to know nothing about these works, and my efforts to find any information about Clark, who appears to have done no other work in Glasgow, were fruitless. Nor was I allowed to take photographs – in case I was planning a robbery, I was informed!

Metal sculpture followed the path already carved out by stone. Planned before World War One, but only completed in the 1920s, the sculptures on the Kelvin Way Bridge by Paul Raphael Montford honour *Commerce and Industry* with a distinctly pre-Raphaelite blacksmith, and *Navigation and Shipbuilding* with a female figure holding a boat belonging closer to the period of Scotland's failed attempt to establish an empire in Darien, than to its position as producer of half the power-driven ships of the British Empire.

Sanitisation of labour occurs even where one might least expect it, on working-class monuments. The People's Palace on Glasgow Green was founded in 1898 as a pioneering museum to the common people of Glasgow, their history and their achievements. Whilst such topics might be acceptable inside the building, they were not for external, public consumption in Victorian times, and the front of the Palace features the now-familiar allegorical female representations of *Shipbuilding, Engineering, and Textile Manufacture*. Even the emerging labour movement eschewed realism and labour as themes, preferring this cloying Victorian habit of sanitising industrial work and workers. The Scottish Co-operative Society buildings were built in Kingston and completed by 1897. These buildings rival the City Chambers in size and almost in magnificence, and here surely was an opportunity to show workers employed in the co-operative labour which was to replace capitalist competition? The Co-op had as examples of such labour several thousand people working not far away at Glasgow's Shieldhall Works, one of the largest co-operative ventures in Europe at this time. But again in the Kingston Co-op we find labour invisible, and the (admittedly splendid) sculptures show instead *Justice* and *Plenty* as buxom, diaphanously clad maidens. It is beyond the scope of social history, but a psychologist might have a plausible theory as to why labour was so often depicted by the Victorians as naked (male) cherubs with visible sexual organs, and by women dressed semi-transparently, with little biological detail – especially mammary detail – left to the imagination.

The sole sculpted exception to this invisibility of labour stands at the main entrance to the offices of the former Fairfield shipyard in Govan, which was constructed in 1888-1890 by the firm of Keppie. Keppie commissioned the Aberdeenshire-born sculptor Pittendrigh MacGillivray to flank the main doorway with life size figures of a *Carpenter* and a *Shipwright*, which appear on the Govan coat of arms. These characters are sympathetically realised (MacGillivray was already attending meetings of the William Morris' Socialist League in Glasgow) and with accuracy in the depiction of the clothing and tools of the men. MacGillivray even shows the social status of each worker in that the carpenter (then considered as being at the apex of shipyard trades) is visibly better dressed and more 'respectable' than the shipwright. But this true representation of the realities of trade remained a virtually isolated case, even in Govan, with its burgh motto *Nihil sine Labore* ('Nothing without Labour'). Much of the sculpture in the burgh before its annexation by Glasgow commemorated the leading shipbuilding magnates, such as Pearce and Elder, and also the latter's wife. In addition there exists another, much cruder, representation of the *Carpenter* and *Shipwright* above the entrance to Govan's Elder Park Library, dating from 1903.

The Govan commission was a one-off for MacGillivray. Though he remained a rather eccentric socialist, none of his later works echoed the realism of this early piece, and MacGillvray left no tradition behind him in Glasgow. It was over a century before the next working man was portrayed in a sculpture in the city. Kenny Hunter's fine *Citizen Firefighter* of 2001 stands outside Central Station, breathing apparatus on, feet in a puddle, his blank visor reflecting his exhaustion. It was erected six months before the 9/11 attacks in New York, and since then has become an unofficial memorial of sorts to that event.

As noted previously, industrial labour was largely hidden underground or behind mill and factory walls. A painter could not stumble upon a proletarian in the same way as he or she might encounter peasant labour whilst wandering the countryside, or in the way the urban *flaneur* might daily encounter the artistic themes of bourgeois life in the city. One had to go and look for industrial labour, and few took the trouble. One artist who did was the Glasgow etcher Muirhead Bone, who produced a fine collection of works on industrial themes. His *Glasgow: Fifty Drawings* (1911) contains some depictions of work at the docks and, perhaps most interestingly, of the smith's shop at the Fairfield's shipyard, but his was not a public art form in the strict sense which I have outlined above.

As in the case of sculpture, the medium of painting provides us with one, and only one, real example of labour as a theme of public art in Victorian Glasgow. A very fine one it is, and from an unexpected artist. Sir John Lavery epitomised the Victorian 'society artist'. Belfast-born and Glasgow-bred, he rose to fame and wealth after he was commissioned to capture Queen Victoria's visit to Glasgow in 1888. He painted the Glasgow bourgeoisie at play, as in *The Tennis Party*, which is set in Cathcart, and executed portraits of eminent people in the Whistler style well into the post-war period. He also painted the Red Clydesider John Maxton's parliamentary portrait between the wars. Reputedly, when Maxton, who was MP for Bridgeton, saw the painting, he insisted Lavery insert industrial scenes into the background, as a sign of where Maxton had originated, and Lavery obliged.

Lavery was one of several artists commissioned after 1888 to paint murals in the banqueting hall of the new City Chambers, and amidst the rather predictable Glasgow Boys' images of St Mungo and the Glasgow Fair, Lavery's is, in my opinion, the most original and interesting. His piece was intended to demonstrate the wealth brought to Glasgow by shipbuilding and, in a unique departure for him, he painted an industrial scene in a shipyard. The yard is Thomson's (later to become the famous John Brown's), which actually lay outside Glasgow city boundaries, in Clydebank. Its workers are shown building a warship for Japan, the men illustrated being minutely depicted in terms of clothing and tools. Of particular interest is the young boy heating rivets on a brazier for the adult tradesmen to use in the ship's construction. If Lavery enjoyed the experience of creating work on this subject, he never repeated it.

A century afterwards, in 1987, one of the New Glasgow Boys, Ken Currie, was commissioned to paint a series of frescoes in the People's Palace depicting the history of the working class in Glasgow. The funding for the project was a bequest from Tommy Chambers, one-time railway worker, lifelong socialist and champion cyclist with 800,000 miles to his credit, and it gave the struggling young Currie, now regarded as one of Scotland's greatest living artists, his first large-scale project and helped make his name. The frescoes are wonderful examples of proletarian art, heavily influenced by the work of the Mexican Diego Rivera rather than by any Scottish artists. Arranged round the roof of the upper floor of the People's Palace, the eight paintings capture the story of the Glasgow working class from the 1787 Calton Weavers Massacre to the UCS Work-In of the early 1970s. We are taken through the Radical War of 1820, the struggles for democratic rights in the Victorian period, the period of Red Clydeside during and after World War One, and the Anti-Fascist struggles of the 1930s.

Most of the panels depict demonstrations or political meetings, with industrial items used as icons or symbols, though *The Socialist Vision, Workers of the World* is mainly set in a foundry. It has in the background a foundry man at his work, but he is largely obscured by a group of his workmates in the foreground forging a motto from the *Communist Manifesto*. The workers are thus tools of artistic didacticism, rather than realistic representatives of working class activity. The panel which depicts the struggle at Upper Clyde Shipbuilders in the early 1970s is the only one to be set in a real industrial location. Although there are lots of tools and other working equipment present in the scene, the men and women shown are having a political discussion during tea-break, and are not actually working! What is important for Currie here is not to depict the work process, but to capture the political unity of the workers across sectarian, gender and craft lines. In Currie's art at the People's Palace, the working class is visible, but labour is not (by comparison, Currie's idol Rivera produced a series of *Detroit Frescoes* of the Ford's motor works in which the workers are actually shown on the assembly lines). This was possibly a missed opportunity from Currie, as one of the objectives of the UCS work-in was to show that without the traditional management structure the workers could, through their collective and co-operative labour, continue to produce the ships that had been already ordered – which they to a great extent succeeded in doing.

Ultimately, it is not in sculpture or painting but in one of the decorative arts that we find the use of labour as a theme in a way which is quite unique. This was the commission given to Stephen Adam to decorate the Maryhill Burgh Halls in 1878 with 20 stained glass panels showing the trades of the burgh, dealt with in detail in Chapter Eight.

Adam's firm did some other industrial-themed work apart from the Maryhill commission. In the former Institute of Engineers and Shipbuilders in Elmbank Street, opened in the early 20th century, they executed an interesting series of stained glass works. These depict famous engineers such as Watt and Rankine and outstanding inventions such as the steam engine and steam locomotion. There is also a panel called *Shipbuilding*, which shows a ship on the stocks with a rather stylised worker in the foreground of the image, bare-chested and with a hammer slung over his shoulder. It is a relatively crude piece of work, and its quality, as with the other items in this collection, comes nowhere near that of the Maryhill panels. Given its late date it may not even be by Adam himself. But, unlike MacGillivray or Lavery with their one-off attempts to give artistic expression to Victorian labour, Adam did leave a legacy of sorts. One of his trainees was William Meikle, who in the 1920s was given the job of working on the War Memorial at the North British Locomotive Works in Springburn commemorating the 300 men from the factory who died in the trenches. Here there are three stained glass panels. Two are fairly conventional, one depicting a soldier, and another showing a classical figure as a blacksmith forging weapons – hardly the way munitions were made at the NBL Co. during World War One. The third panel is the most interesting in that it shows a female munitions worker operating a lathe. Again the detail is fine: her buckled shoes, protective head-covering etc. reflect reality and an attention to detail rarely seen elsewhere. The lathe, too, is well described – only Meikle was no engineer, for it is shown as left-handed, and just as there are no left-handed screwdrivers, there are no left-handed lathes. Nevertheless, this is a fine piece of work. The woman's solemn expression may suggest to the viewer some close personal connection to one of the 300 men killed on active service and commemorated here.

More recently, in 1997, a set of stained glass windows in the style of Stephen Adam were designed for the *Lismore* public house in Partick. These capture various scenes of Highland life and the Clearances. Two depict workmen, one showing a pair of coopers, and another a blacksmith. But these are historicist stained glass works set in the Highlands of 150 years ago rather than, as Adam's Maryhill works and those of Meikle were, ones depicting contemporary workmen and women.

I would like to conclude by returning to my main theme of the general invisibility of labour in public art and by drawing attention to the depiction of the fishing industry on a gorgeous tiled panel by James Duncan from a fish shop on the South Side of Glasgow, created in 1894. Generations of Glaswegians must have enjoyed their fish suppers all the more knowing that each fish was individually caught by such a fishwife, a maiden of such classical beauty and garb that the fish must have leapt from the water to be caught by her fair hands. The panel is currently on display in the People's Palace.

Public art underwent a general decline in the 20th century compared with its popularity in Victorian times (though the last couple of decades have seen modest signs of a revival in the genre). Despite the rise of the labour movement, not much of the art produced in the last century reflected the aspirations of labour, or showed its supporters in their daily working lives. Glasgow's most celebrated public sculptor in the 20th century was probably the Russian-born Benno Schotz. He relates in his autobiography, *Bronze in my Blood* (1981), how he came to Glasgow to work as an engineer in John Brown's Clydebank shipyard before World War One. Despite this industrial-technical background, and despite Schotz seeing thousands of working men at their daily labours as he spent over a decade working in Brown's, Schotz' sculpture never dealt with the theme of labour. Ignorance therefore cannot be a justification for the exclusion of the subject from his work, and we must find another reason why he might have wished to leave his industrial background behind him.

Whether they were ignorant of labour, felt guilty about worker exploitation, were frightened by the working class, or whether they were simply uninspired by the issue of industrial work as a topic, artists in Glasgow have largely ignored labour as a theme of public art over the last two centuries. In the case of labour and its representation in public art as exemplified by Glasgow, we can say without much fear of contradiction that seldom can so many, to whom society owed so much, have been commemorated by so few, which makes what examples we do have of this commemoration so much more valuable.

Notes on Sites

Glasgow City Chambers is located centrally on George Square, and is usually open for free tours daily at 10.30am and 2.30pm. The Stock Exchange is a short distance to the west of George Square at Nelson Mandela Square and the former Commercial Bank is nearby in Gordon Street. The People's Palace is a little further out of the centre, on Glasgow Green, but easily walkable from George Square (15 minutes). Open daily between 10am–5pm, (Sundays 2pm–5pm). The restored Doulton Fountain stands outside the People's Palace.

Fairfield shipyard (now BAE Systems) lies five minutes west of Govan Cross, which can be reached in ten minutes by subway from Buchanan Street, off George Square. The North British Locomotive Co. offices (now workspace/business units) are five minutes from Springburn station, which is itself 15 minutes from Queen Street station at George Square. Access is normally allowed to visitors during working hours.

Possil Basin.
A former industrial berthage on the Forth and Clyde Canal, which was used as a location for the filming of *Young Adam*. Now the headquarters of Scottish Canals, which manages the reopened and regenerated canal.

Great Western Terrace.
Probably the architect Alexander 'Greek' Thomson's domestic masterpiece, from 1870. One of the houses was occupied by William Burrell. The terrace stood in for the residences of the New York plutocracy in the film *House of Mirth*.

Clay Pipe Works, Calton.

Originally designed to be built in stone, costs dictated a scale down to brick, but nevertheless an interesting and exuberant construction with its bay windows and coloured brickwork. Partially converted to flats.

Daily Express Building.

Often misnamed The Herald Building as that paper later replaced the original occupant for whom it was designed by Owen Williams in the 1930s. Black Vitrolite round a steel frame, brash and bold Art Deco. Now apartments.

Shipbuilding on the Clyde.
By Sir John Lavery. Located in the banqueting hall of the Glasgow City Chambers this painting is unique in its subject, both for the artist and for the time (c.1899) in that it depicts industrial labour in detail, down to the heating of rivets by a young worker.
© *CSG CIC Glasgow Museums Collection*

Maiden, Stock Exchange.
Engineering here is represented by a classic damsel holding a cogwheel, a sanitised version of industrial production.

Citizen Firefighter, Central Station.
Kenny Hunter's work from 2001 is fine study of an exhausted fireman standing blankly in a puddle of water, and was the first statue to commemorate a working man in Glasgow for over a century.

Hunterian Museum And Memorial, Glasgow University.
The memorial, with bronze reliefs by GH Paulin, to the 'brother surgeons' William and John Hunter, the greatest British physicians of the eighteenth century. The Hunterian Museum lies behind.

Courtesy of Patrick Harley

Lord Kelvin, Kelvin Way.

Statue of William Thomson by Shannan from 1913 when the scientist, recently buried in Westminster Abbey, was at the height of his renown. The sculptor worked a model of Kelvin's marine compass into the back of the statue.

Courtesy of Patrick Harley

Cyril Gerber Fine Art Gallery, Blythswood Hill.

The most recent location of the various galleries associated for more than 50 years with Cyril Gerber, who did much to promote art in Glasgow and Glasgow's artists in that time.

The Pearce Institute, Govan.

Designed by Rowand Anderson and built 1902–5, in an eclectic mix of Scottish and Flemish Renaissance styles, with much exterior decoration. A social and recreational club for working men and women, often dubbed 'The Heart of Govan'.

Ibrox Park, Govan (South Stand).

Archibald Leitch, architect of many of Britain's football stadia built no grander sporting temple than this A-Listed masterpiece from 1929, for Rangers, the club he supported. Alex Ferguson had a troubled time here as a player.

Grand Ole Opry, Govan Road.

In an unprepossessing former cinema can be found a piece of the Old Wild West, Glasgow's home of country and western Americana, complete with cowboys and cowgals, shoot outs – and cheap beer and 'chuck'.

Courtesy of Patrick Harley

La Passionara, Clyde Street.

Recently renovated memorial by Arthur Dooley, to the Spanish Communist leader, Dolores Ibarutti ('La Passionara') and to the Glasgow volunteers for the International Brigades who fought in the Spanish Civil War in the 1930s.

Boyd Orr Building, University Avenue.

A 1970s glass and concrete construction commemorating Lord Boyd Orr, graduate from and later Chancellor of, the University, founding member of the campaign for Nuclear Disarmament, and winner of the Nobel Peace Prize.

Courtesy of Patrick Harley

The Sawmill Worker, Maryhill.

This stained glass panel from the Burgh Halls by Stephen Adam shows, inadvertantly, how many ways this man could be injured or killed. No protective clothing, no guards on the machinery, no guards on the drive belting…

Courtesy of Glasgow Life

CHAPTER SIX

Joan Eardley's Townhead

SOME URBAN AREAS become synonymous with particular great artists, for obvious reasons. The example of Utrillo who made Paris' Montmartre district his own comes to mind, but there are few comparables in Scotland, to my knowledge. Stanley Spencer certainly captured many of the shipyards, houses and people of Port Glasgow during World War Two and afterwards, but they represented his idealised Port Glasgow, not the grim reality. Joan Eardley, however, represents the clear relationship between an urban artist and the distinct *habitus* of their work, which in her case was the Townhead district of Glasgow. But while the modern day tourist can see Utrillo's Montmartre almost as he painted it, if any visitors were to wander into modern Townhead, behind the shopping malls and university buildings which now surround the district, they would find that little remains to remind us of Eardley's unique vision of half a century ago.

I thought I knew Joan Eardley's work, having loved the sea and landscape paintings she did in the North East village of Catterline (where she lived intermittently in the 1950s), but the 2007 major retrospective of her work (held, rather perversely, to my mind, in The National Gallery in Edinburgh, rather than in Glasgow) showed the error of my ways by revealing just how central to her was the time she spent in her Townhead studio and the works she painted there. The exhibition resulted in a wonderful and quickly-reprinted catalogue, containing not only many of her Townhead paintings, but also several photographs, including some which she took herself of the district in the late 1940s and 1950s. This publication, *Joan Eardley* by Fiona Pearson, with its mixture of paintings and photographs, is a good starting point for discovering what Townhead was like over half a century ago, before it vanished (with the exception of a few public buildings) almost without trace in the Comprehensive Redevelopment approach to Glasgow's housing issues in the wake of World War Two, which envisaged the demolition of most of the City's Victorian tenement areas, deemed to be slums.

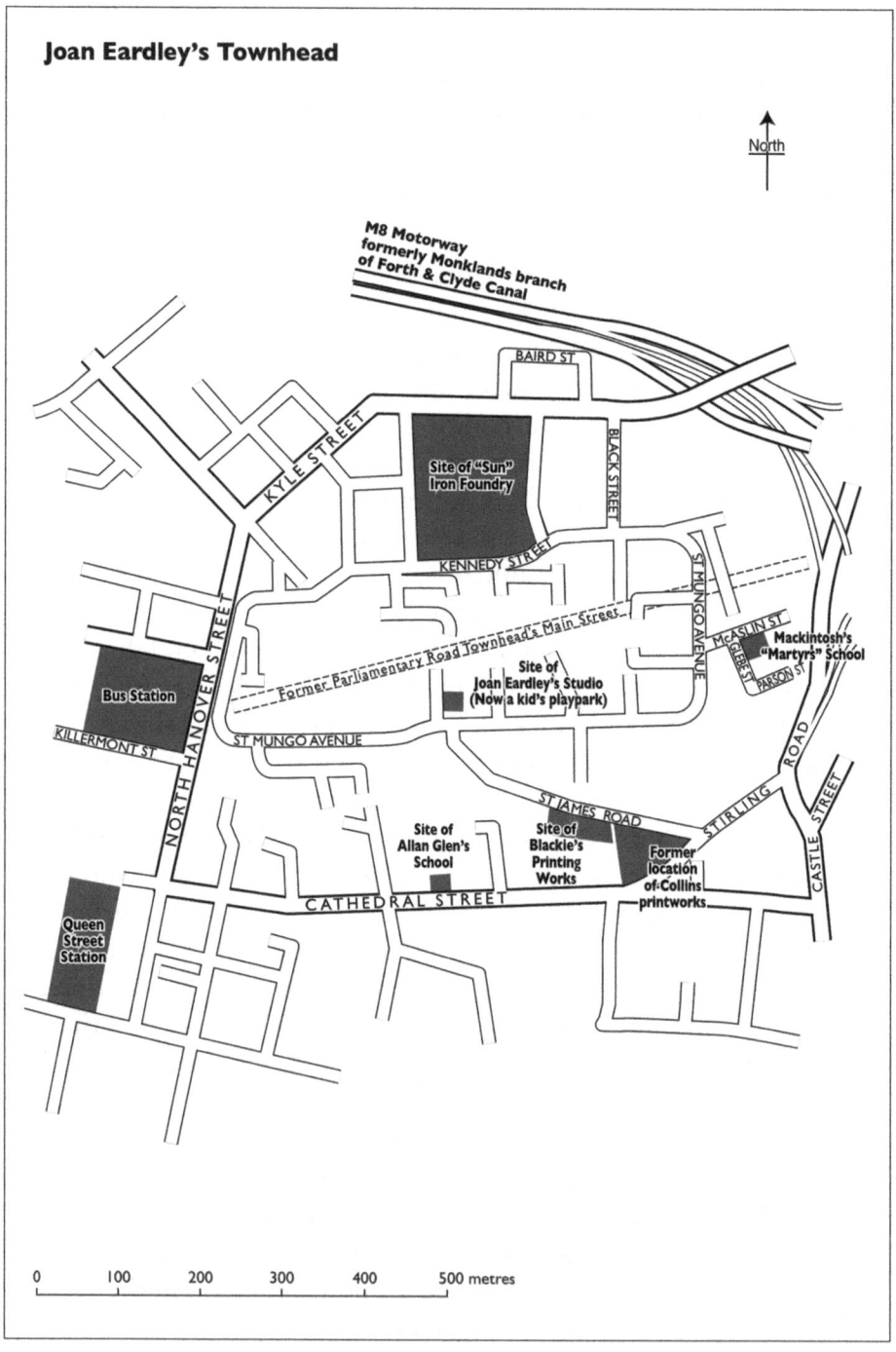

Eardley's Townhead was similar to many inner-city Glasgow slum areas at that time, alike to Cowcaddens, North Woodside and the Gorbals in being an area of exceptional overcrowding in generally poor quality tenement blocks. What marked Townhead apart from these other slum areas was its close proximity to the city centre, starting at the rear entrance of Queen Street Station, just two minutes from Glasgow's George Square and the City Chambers. From there it stretched eastwards towards Glasgow Cathedral and the High Street. Avoid other slums as they might, Glasgow's more affluent citizens could hardly avoid knowing Townhead. Indeed, many of their suburban male offspring attended the prestigious Allan Glen's School, which then lay on Townhead's southern periphery.

Bounded to the north by the Forth and Clyde canal (now by the M8 motorway), to the east by High Street and Castle Street, to the south by Rottenrow, the western gateway to Townhead was Parliamentary Road where it left Cowcaddens between the portals of Queen Street Station and the now long gone Buchanan Street Goods Station. Much of this western area has disappeared under the Buchanan Street Shopping Centre, the Buchanan Bus Station and the expanding campus of Caledonian University. Today a realigned and much extended North Hanover Street is the western 'border' of Townhead.

As was the case in other inner-city, largely unskilled working class areas in Glasgow, there was then a great problem with overcrowding amongst Townhead's 35,000 people. Though not as densely inhabited as some areas, in 1951 the population per acre in Townhead was 116 against a city average of 27. As was the case with many poor areas, the tenement 'closes' opened straight onto the street, with no gardens, railings or other decorative features. The main thoroughfare was the long, straight stretch of Parliamentary Road which bisected Townhead and ran from the railway stations in the west to the canal in the east. Not a single house on this street escaped demolition, and even the street name and its line are gone in the tenement-free Townhead of today. I recall being dropped off at one end of this street in the mid-1960s, having hitch-hiked from Aberdeen, and then walking to Queen Street Station. Aside from the multi-story towers rising from the ashes it looked like images I had seen of bombed Berlin; huge areas of dereliction, broken by the odd block of blackened tenements awaiting demolition, characterised the Townhead area.

Close to the canal, which was still operating in the 1950s, and the city centre, warehousing and stabling were amongst the main employments; though declining, the use of horses was still widespread, and horse dung might have been one of the pleasanter smells in the area. The largest heavy industrial concern was just north of the canal. This was the St Rollox chemical works, once the largest in Europe, but now downsizing, closed and demolished in the mid-1960s. Most interesting, however, was the concentration of printing works in Townhead. The original Glasgow University Printing Press, later taken over by Blackie's Publishers, was in Stanhope Street, whilst on Cathedral Street stood the works of religious and temperance printer Collins. Glasgow's greatest Victorian monument sculptors, Mossman and Co, had their workshop on Cathedral Street, originally sited there in order to be close to the Necropolis. Most of these industries were still operating when Eardley moved to Townhead in 1950. The next year's census recorded Glasgow's highest ever population at well over one million, and ideas of its later industrial and population decline were still far from many people's thoughts.

Eardley took a studio on the corner of McAslin Street and St James' Road. She kept this base in Townhead until her death in 1963, returning frequently even after moving to Catterline in 1955, and working in the studio almost daily in the period 1950–1955. English-born Eardley came to Glasgow in 1939 aged 18, and studied at the Glasgow School of Art. Though she came from a middle class background and lived in the loftier heights of the Bearsden suburb, Eardley encountered working class life as a joiner's labourer during the Second World War, painting camouflage on landing craft in the boatyard at Kelvin Dock in Maryhill. Interestingly, while she was painting the boats, another artist, Franc Martin, was painting the industrial scene at the dock. During the Second World War Eardley met the Jewish artist and refugee Josef Herman in his Glasgow studio, and it is clear his strong images of working people had an influence on her later work, as it seems did the work of Stanley Spencer in Port Glasgow, where she herself painted in later years.

Eardley responded best to scenes of demotic street life in Glasgow. She loved the city and talked of 'this richness that Glasgow has – I hope it will always have – a living thing, intense quality... as long as Glasgow has this I will always want to paint'. Early canvases reflect this, recording a poverty stricken *Street Market* selling second-hand clothes, street life in *Back Street Bookie*, in which a child acts as lookout for the police, and images of working people, such as the road builders in *Mixer Men*. Though she had left-wing sympathies, Eardley's paintings are not propagandist, seeking the human touch rather than the social message.

It was in Townhead that she immersed herself in the colours and rhythms of working class life, which she found especially stimulating. Though in some ways Joan was a lonely and depressive individual, she responded with alacrity to life around her, and particularly to the children of the area, with their colourful patched clothes and limitless energy. She always carried a camera, partly because the children were so lively that it was difficult to make them pose, and she used the photographs for her paintings. The paintings of the 1950–55 period are a rich record of the children of Townhead, and the slum buildings are never more than a backdrop to the picture. She shows the kids' mismatched multi-coloured clothing, their squints, their missing teeth, humour and camaraderie. They can be seen playing with skipping ropes, dolls, marbles, and games chalked on pavements; a whole array of activities that are almost totally forgotten now.

There was little precedent for the work of Joan Eardley in Glasgow. The main 'School' of Glasgow painters, the Glasgow Boys, had painted mostly rural landscapes and people. It is true that Muirhead Bone, in his *Fifty Glasgow Drawings* and elsewhere, had etched the city and its industries, but the focus for him was the buildings and industries rather than the people. With Eardley it was always the people, especially the children, who formed the main focus of her paintings. Eardley became especially friendly with the children of one family, the Samsons, saying 'there are a large number of them, twelve… they amuse me – they are full of what's going on today – who's broken into what shop and who's flung a pie in who's face… they are Glasgow'. In their turn, the kids appeared to enjoy being Eardley's models. Mary Samson later recalled how they 'loved her studio. It was like a treasure trove with nooks and crannies everywhere to play'. Given presents of sketches, she confesses they made paper aeroplanes out of them when they got home and that their mother, Jean, used them as spills to light the fire.

Jean Samson was still alive in 2010 and, alongside her daughters Mary and Anne, was interviewed on television and in the press. It is clear that Jean's main motivation was to get a break, especially in school holidays, from the pressures of child-minding, and she was delighted to have her progeny spend time in Eardley's studio. On occasion the artist even took Andrew, her favourite sitter, to Catterline with her on holiday.

However, the Samson Maw was by no means impressed by Eardley's drawings, which she felt were unflattering, and not how a respectable working class mother in the 1950s liked to see her children depicted, with squints, scuffed shoes and torn clothes. She candidly commented:

> Andrew was always in Joan's studio. He was the first and then she came to the house and asked if she could take the rest of them. It was seven week's holiday and I was just glad to get rid of them for a wee while. They'd bring paintings home and scatter them about the house and I used to tear them up and throw them in the fire. It was after she had died the lawyer asked if we had any sketches. We'd burned millions. When we saw Joan's paintings in the Art Gallery and we saw our Andrew, I said 'don't let everybody know' because I thought they were horrible.
>
> *The Herald* 29 September 2012

Eardley's work can now sell for up to £200,000 a canvas, and she was critically acclaimed during her short life (she died aged 42), but at the time she sold few works and even then, only cheaply. Though one exhibition in London in 1963 was a great success, for most of her artistic life she appears to have lived largely off modest investments left to her by her family. Maw Samson could have been a millionaire had she kept Eardley's drawings, and her kids who made paper aeroplanes of them probably regret this too, but the Samsons grew up in the post-war period of plentiful employment, education and the welfare state. They all appear to have done reasonably well in life, in spite of any difficulties their childhood may have contained. Can we be as confident that the children of Townhead today face such a prospect of an improving future?

When Eardley was painting in Townhead, it was composed, as it had been for three quarters of a century, of factories and tenements, though the latter were in a much decayed condition. However cosy they may have been inside, photographs of the Townhead tenements from Eardley's camera and those of others show that, by the 1950s, the fabric of these buildings was in a very poor state. By the mid-1960s all of Townhead's tenements were gone, with a completeness achieved in no other Comprehensive Redevelopment Area, where occasionally a better street was left, or even an isolated superior quality building. Townhead's tenements were replaced by medium-and high-rise housing of much lower population density, and many of the streets themselves disappeared. Parliamentary Road, once the main thoroughfare of the area, is no longer on the map, and several other streets remain only in truncated fragments. Anyone trying to find Eardley's Townhead would need a pre-1955 street atlas. One or two public buildings remain, such as the two secondary schools, but they are both closed and only a primary remains to serve a population of about 5,000 people.

What fascinates me most about this radical change to Glasgow's landscape is that Joan Eardley saw the redevelopment happening, but did not respond to it artistically. She continued to paint until 1963, but the paintings are identical in theme and format to those she was executing ten or more years earlier. Townhead, by comparison, was not; by the early 1960s much had already been demolished, many of the remaining tenements were empty, and the foundations of a new housing situation were well underway. I suspect that Eardley – who probably knew she was dying – tried to ignore this, given how important to her integration within the Townhead community had been at an earlier stage in her life. In the early 1960s she gave an interview in which she mused that 'the community feeling is rapidly disappearing in Glasgow... I do feel there is still a little bit left. I still try and paint Glasgow as long as there is this'. This was a place that had given a lonely, depressive person, and one frequently in severe pain through illness, so much human warmth.

If you were to look for any remains of Eardley's Townhead, you might arrive at Queen Street Station, and head up North Hanover Street, noting the lost lands of Townhead on the left, until you join the now much truncated Dobbies Loan. Around Dobbies Loan and the adjacent Kyle and Baird Streets were located many of the area's industries. Much of the land around here is now given over to student accommodation for Caledonian University, as well as to the University itself. Kennedy Street divides the warehousing and small industrial units to the north from the modern housing to the south. Here stood the Sun Foundry, makers of high-quality cast iron products, and just past this at Lister Street is located the Council's Bowling Green, virtually the only open space in Eardley's Townhead, now restored as a social asset after long lying derelict. The most notable factory hereabouts, in vanished Murray Street, was probably Rattray's Cycles, makers of the famous *Flying Scot* bike. At Glebe Street things now come pretty much to a stop amongst motorway flyovers and slipways, but in Eardley's time Kennedy Street continued past the public Wash House and the police and fire stations to Townhead Library, all now disappeared beneath the torrent of the M8, along with the associated housing. Here also were the two local cinemas, one of them probably the setting for Eardley's *Saturday Matinee Picture Queue*.

If we continue down Glebe Street we come to Charles Rennie Mackintosh's Martyrs' Public School, almost demolished for the motorway and only saved by a furious protest campaign, now perched perilously above the traffic flow. Built a decade before his much more famous Scotland Street School, this is early Mackintosh, possibly not yet as assured as he was later to be, but a significant cultural icon nevertheless. Originally built to commemorate two Protestant Reformation adherents martyred in 1537, shifting demography meant that for a while, ironically, it became a Roman Catholic school. Today it is a Glasgow Museums resource centre, occasionally open to the public. Many of the children Eardley painted would have attended the Martyrs' School.

Crossing the busy Stirling Road and heading southwards, you reach the only housing in the whole of Townhead that Eardley would recognise. Standing here in isolation is a block of solid 1930s Glasgow Corporation slum clearance houses which has remained whilst all else around have fallen. They lie on Cathedral Street and the Mossman Monumental Sculpture works could formerly be found on the site next door, now occupied by an Evangelical church. But before we head up what remains of St James Road, we should take a look a little further down Castle Street.

Eardley was not drawn to paint what generations of artists saw as one of Glasgow's most picturesque buildings. The city's oldest house, Provand's Lordship, was not her aesthetic. The Lordship stands just south of here at the junction of Castle Street and Macleod Street. Built in the late 15th century as a hospital, the building underwent many uses, including as a public house, until settling down as part of an overcrowded slum area. It also saw several alterations, but restoration works since the 1980s have rendered it an effective museum with a delightful herb garden out back.

Returning to Stirling Street we find ourselves in the ever-expanding territories of Strathclyde University, which adopted this name in 1964 (Joan would have known it as the Glasgow and West of Scotland Royal Technical College). Originally centred on George Street, the institution expanded north and east, taking in everything up to Cathedral Street, including the infamous slum area of Rottenrow (Rotten = rattan, old Scots for rat), which was formerly the location of Glasgow's maternity hospital. Eardley painted in the Rottenrow that was part of *her* Townhead, but today it is decidedly city-centre and university territory, student flats replacing the crowded pre-industrial 'lands' which still partially remained in the 1950s. North of Cathedral Street another cluster of colleges, recently amalgamated to form City of Glasgow College, blocked further Strathclyde expansion in that direction. But Collins Printing Works, still going strong in Eardley's time, closed down in 1978 and the land became the Curran Building of the University. This was re-faced in brick, with slit windows, and forms a striking if not entirely pleasing junction between St James Road and Cathedral Street.

Collins was, at its height, one of the largest printing and publishing firms in the world. Its owners were leading figures in Glasgow life and politics, William Collins acting as Provost from 1877–1880. They made their fortune printing bibles before they diversified to diaries and more general publishing. They were model employers who built the Collins Institute (a social and health and welfare club for their employees) near to their works; this too has disappeared with the expansion of Strathclyde's campus. In 1950 they employed 2,500 people here, but it is unlikely that many of the printing workers employed by Collins lived in the crowded slums of Townhead. Serving a long apprenticeship, print workers were highly skilled, highly unionised and highly paid. They were the aristocrats of the proletarian aristocracy.

Further up St James' Road we pass the partial remains of Blackie's Villafield Printworks. Blackie anticipated Collins by several decades, moving his works to Bishopbriggs in 1930. Blackie's former works retain a link with printing as the location of the joint Glasgow and Strathclyde Universities' Printworks. Beyond this we are near where Eardley's studio once stood, at the junction of St James' Road with McAslin Street. But do not go looking for the building which housed it – or even its former site – for St James' Road used to join with Dobbies Loan on Parliamentary Road; it now ends abruptly in a new street know as St Mungo's Avenue. Somewhere to the north of this there is a pedestrian walkway which vaguely follows the line of the former Parliamentary Road. My estimation of where Eardley's studio was formerly located is precisely the point at which a modern children's playground is to be found. I am sure Eardley would have liked that.

I attempted some time ago, through a series of meetings, to interest the Byzantine structure of councillors, town planners and others to develop some form of commemoration to Eardley in Townhead, but, alas, she has a serious rival as a local icon. Charles Rennie Mackintosh was born in Townhead and his Martyrs' Church, built near his birthplace, is still there, as noted above. A splendid series of Mackintosh-inspired public sculptures, designed with the help of local children, line the pedestrian walkway through Townhead. I have nothing against Mackintosh, whom the Council appears to be promoting as the city's main icon, but Mackintosh mania is in danger of squeezing out due recognition for other artists, like Eardley, who have also worked in the city. It seems possible that some kind of memorial to Eardley could be executed in the newly built Townhead Village Community Centre, to commemorate her links with the area, which I am sure that Joan would have appreciated. Her work, and the deep sympathy of that work's vision, is almost all we have left of the Townhead of half a century ago.

Hemmed in by motorways and sandwiched between two expanding universities, Joan Eardley's Townhead has shrunk markedly from its former dimensions. What remains shows almost no physical resemblance to the place she knew and which inspired her art. The whole of the remaining Townhead has recently been upgraded in the housing and public space realms, but it remains a world or two away from the high-tech universities and fashionable retail outlets which now surround it. Whilst no-one would claim that this area is some sort of urban Eden, I am sure that much of the community Eardley feared was being lost has resurfaced in new forms in the Townhead that has replaced the one she knew.

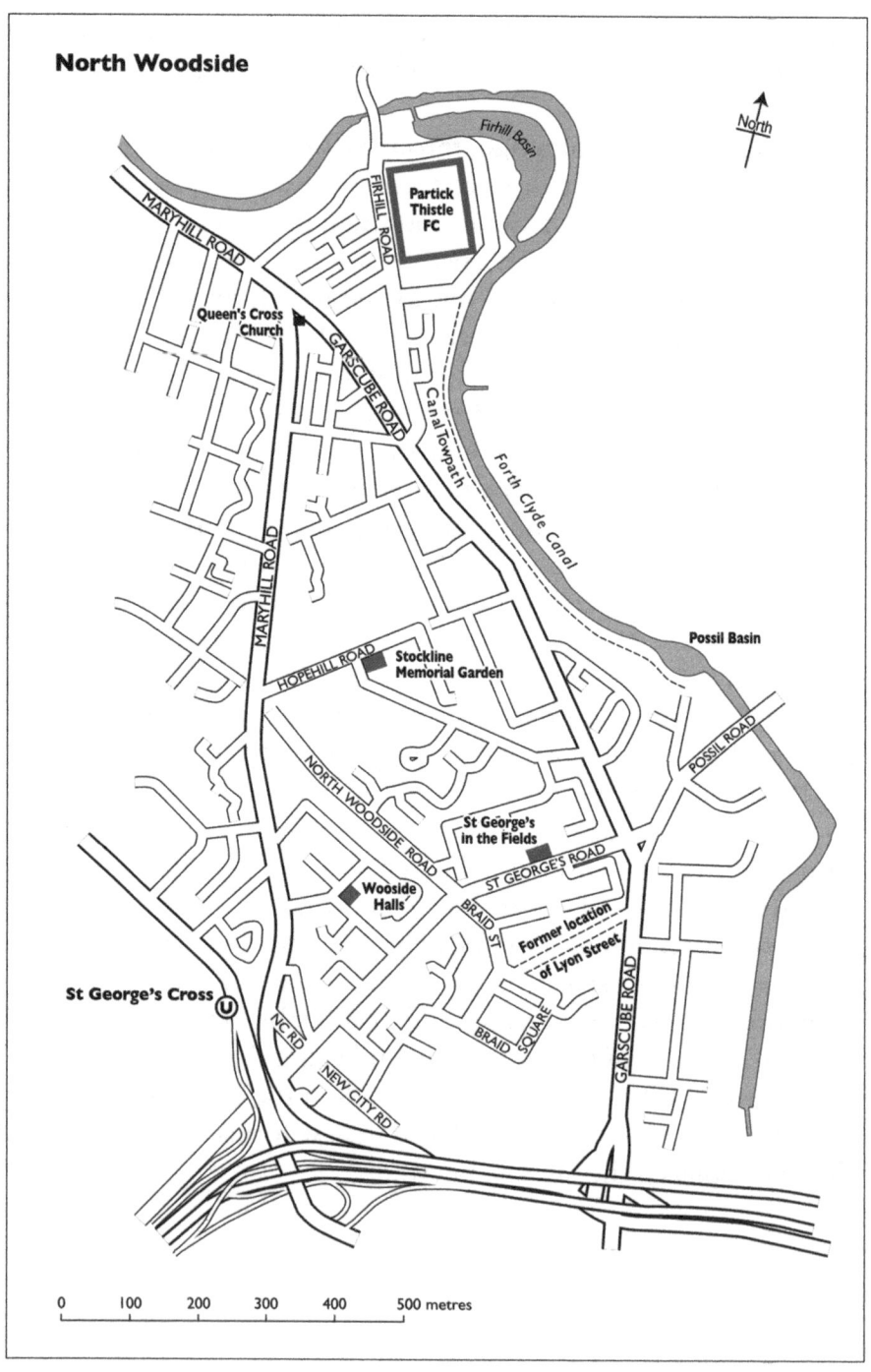

CHAPTER SEVEN

North Woodside: Iconography of a Forgotten Quarter

WOODSIDE IS A place name which is in danger of disappearing from Glasgow's geography, both mentally and physically. Urban redevelopment means that people's concept of what is meant by a particular area can expand – but it can wither as well. Nowadays North Woodside is regarded as part of Greater Maryhill, and the lower section of Maryhill Road certainly runs through it. But, as a Woodside patriot put it to me in the local swimming baths one day, 'London Road isnae in London, and Maryhill Road isnae in Maryhill'. He has a valid point. Maryhill Road here was formerly called New City Road, and many older locals resent the changed designation, which makes the thoroughfare a conduit for Maryhill expansionism. I live close to North Woodside and use its facilities frequently. Within this chapter, I hope to repay any debt thus incurred by helping to ensure that this 'forgotten quarter' remains on the map. Woodside has certainly seen hard times but today, though no Hampstead, it is in better heart than in former years.

North Woodside has a very distinct geographical delineation, as clear and compact as a Parisian *quartier*. It straddles the triangle made by the lower Maryhill Road heading north-west from St George's Cross to Queen's Cross, where it turns south, occupying both sides of the Garscube Road until it reaches what was formerly known as Garscube Toll, and there reconnects with St George's Cross, the 'hinge' of the area, via the territories on either side of St George's Road. The former southern boundary, New City Road, has all but disappeared under the expanding M8 motorway.

The 1958 *Statistical Account of Glasgow* (SAOG) indicates that North Woodside was a distinct entity; though the city's smallest council ward by area (170 acres), it was home at that time over 27,000 inhabitants. The *SAoG* reveals that this amounted to the highest density of population then in the city, at 158 persons to the acre. This was a density greater even than that of the Gorbals, which had at least a couple of green spaces where North Woodside had none. This density of population is evinced by a comparison to the city average at that time, which was a mere 27 persons to the acre.

John Hume's *Industrial Archaeology of Glasgow* provides a picture of local employment in Woodside in former days. At that time there was a great variety of industries in the area, almost all of them small-scale, and many highly polluting, such as chrome manufacture, bleaching, and iron foundries. Few areas benefited, or suffered, depending on your point of view, from Comprehensive Redevelopment as much as North Woodside. The vast majority of the tenement buildings in Woodside were demolished, and almost all of the industry was either relocated or simply went out of business. Nevertheless, 50 years on the area retains its historical interest, as represented by the many fine public – and some industrial – buildings which survived redevelopment, and also by pockets of what were the better tenements and even townhouses from the pre-industrial era. Some of these buildings help to retain vestiges of a Woodside identity in the face of Maryhill expansionism by boasting the Woodside name. Let's start our tour at the Front Line, the interface of North Woodside with Maryhill at Queen's Cross.

Though a largely forgotten quarter, North Woodside contains one of Glasgow's most visited monuments, the iconic Charles Rennie Mackintosh Queen's Cross Church. This, the headquarters of the Mackintosh Society, was the only church the architect ever completed, and it is now generally regarded as being situated in Maryhill. However, when the church was built for the Free Kirk in 1899, it was unambiguously in Glasgow. The former burgh of Maryhill, later annexed by Glasgow, did not start until a couple of streets further north of this site. It saddens me a little that the thousands who come here on their Mackintosh pilgrimage never seem to venture further, to form a picture of the area and learn about the people 'Toshie' built this church for – for there is plenty to see. Places of pilgrimage should be a stepping stone rather than an end in themselves.

Before we leave, take a look around at the housing built here as part of the Maryhill Corridor project in the 1980s and later 1990s. Whilst Comprehensive Redevelopment went too far in demolition and its own housing solutions were not always above criticism, there existed in areas like North Woodside an undeniable problem of overcrowding and poor housing which simply had to be tackled. The housing conditions in this area were amongst the worst in Glasgow; look at what has replaced them without the starry eyed *sterrheid* nostalgia for yesteryear and there is no doubt that things, at least as far as housing conditions are concerned, are better here today than they were.

However, for some local institutions, it seems that there is still room to improve. Partick Thistle FC are a strange – and welcome – non-sectarian phenomenon in a city dominated by the tribal loyalties of Rangers and Celtic. They are also strange in that they have not played in Partick – despite retaining the name – for over a century. People of a certain age may recall that when in the 1950s the Hungarians were the most exciting team in the world, Partick were dubbed by those of an ironic disposition 'The Maryhill Magyars'. Wrong again, for 'they're nae in Partick, nor in Maryhill neither', according to my swimming pundit. Partick relocated here to Firhill Stadium, which is on the Glasgow – *not* Maryhill – side of the Forth and Clyde Canal, this being the former boundary between city and burgh. A short walk from the Mackintosh Church and we stand outside the pleasing stand built by The Thistle in 1927, which sports an appropriate thistle emblem. Perversity still brings me to Firhill occasionally, to watch what should be Woodside Thistle or the Woodside Magyars – though I accept these names don't have much ring to them.

Behind Firhill is a development of student flats (the proceeds of which probably saved the football club from liquidation some years back), and the canal path which provides a grand belvedere over North Woodside as we head down along the banks. Firhill Basin lies behind the stadium, home to a great concentration of canal-side industry in former days. Excavated in 1799 and extended in 1849, the basin was the site of iron foundries and chemical works, and, perhaps most importantly, it was the centre of Glasgow's timber industry, where the raw materials were brought by canal barge to the sawmills which cluttered the banks. Today the last vestiges of industry are gone, and whilst some land is being given over to housing developments, most of the area remains a wilderness, overgrown and filled with incredible wildlife. On a fine day, with its view over the city, this is undoubtedly one of the loveliest places in Glasgow.

On the north canal bank the wild land around Firhill Basin merges into Westercommon. This is also a wild and overgrown inner-city habitat, the last of Glasgow's common lands. Since it is across the canal in Possil, we will concentrate instead on what we can see from North Woodside 'proper'. The canal supports swans, coots and goosanders, and on its banks more ornithology is offered by the dookits – pigeon lofts constructed by some of the city's legion of pigeon-fanciers. If we are looking for icons, these dookits certainly qualify. We look down here on the Garscube Road, or what remains of it after much demolition and as it is slowly being filled by new housing developments. Indeed, all the old housing on the north side of the road ('The Gaspipe' as it was known locally) is gone, leaving the odd stunted derelict pub and other ruins. The Gaspipe was North Woodside 'improper', the roughest and toughest place in the area, consisting of bad housing juxtaposed with polluting industries. There was, for example, a chrome works situated amongst the housing, as well as an iron foundry.

In his lovely book *The Scots-Italians*, Joe Pieri writes of the Italian immigrants setting up fish and chip shops here in the early 20th century. The first location an Italian child learned to find was that of the local police station, and the first words taught were 'big fight in fish shop'. But the Italians were not only the victims of this culture; some of their black sheep became mini-*Mafiosi* themselves. Pieri tells of Tony Biagi, a street bookie and re-setter who was deported to Italy, and of Laurie Ventre, another who practised these trades but who also had the reputation of paying the debts of needy local people. The importance of such characters to this area is

Canal Towpath.
Approaching Possil Basin in former days, the canal-side crowded with industry, and with the Great Maltings dominant in the leftbackground. (J. Brown, 1923).

captured by Pieri, who notes how Ventre's 'death in the 1960s was mourned by a funeral to rival that of any Chicago Godfather, with cartloads of flowers and hundreds of mourners who afterwards set new records for liquor consumed in local pubs'.

All along the Garscube Road by the canal there are still gap sites and derelict land where once stood factories, like the sadly-demolished Great Canal Maltings, the biggest of many such in the city, and once a fine brick building with a pagoda adorned roof. The Master Plan for the redevelopment of the Forth and Clyde Canal sees the regeneration of 'The Gaspipe' in its restoration as a main thoroughfare, with new housing occupying the vacant land by the canal which is currently occupied by 'landscaped' sites. As is often the case in inner cities, these are 'dead lands' which support only some spindly trees and much rubbish.

Woodside is also home to several fine churches, and looking across Garscube Road from the canal path, one such comes into view which merits a short side trip. This is St Columba's RC Church, built between 1937 and 1941, one of the first such commissions of the uncompromisingly modernist firm of Gillespie, Kidd and Coia: the Jew, the Protestant and the Atheist responsible for much of the Catholic Church's west of Scotland architecture. While Mackintosh's style looked backwards, this firm embraced modernism and all its materials, such as concrete, with plain brick walls inside and out. St Columba's contains a crucifix by Benno Schotz. The church, which was expensive to build, was reputedly paid for by local parishioners buying bricks at a halfpenny each. A sign outside the church tells of this incredible devotion, which, amongst other things, indicates how densely populated this area was back in 1940. It takes a lot of folk to build a church at a halfpenny per brick. Perhaps the most generous of these souls bought two or three...

The delightful Applecross or Possil Basin soon comes into view. This is the headquarters of Scottish Canals and usually hosts a varied flotilla of SC craft, tourist barges and other boats. The observant explorer will notice that not only do many of the buildings date from the 1790s, when the basin was constructed, but also that here the canal towpath is laid with rough cobblestones of that period. Further on is a former bonded warehouse, whose previously blank brick walls are now punctuated with windows, with the building converted into artists' studios. Dropping down Baird's Brae brings you to what was formerly Garscube Toll, or what the locals sometimes call 'The Round Tower', after a striking building still standing there. The Tower looks like a tenement building but was actually constructed in 1875 as offices for an iron foundry, and today contains a variety of small enterprises, sporting clubs and the like. It is not an overly impressive building, but it is interesting, and renovating it would provide a central feature in any future redevelopment of the area. It might even be reopened under the auspices of its heyday function; until the 1950s one of its storeys, which has a suspended floor, was given over to dancing as the Tower Ballroom.

Travelling down St George's Road, the quality of development improves considerably and there is much to see. On our left (to the east) lies the North Woodside Estate, which was constructed in the 1970s in bold brick medium-rise lines intended to echo tenement architecture. This is a successful housing development with a real sense of community, as anyone visiting the Woodside Baths, which lie in the heart of the scheme, will discover. Ideas of inner-city alienation can be over-stated. When I started patronising these baths, everyone knew everyone, except me. But I was soon accepted as a suitable recipient for the dishing-out of local punditry. The baths and washhouse were constructed in the 1880s when few here had washing facilities, and it is the only remaining building in the area from pre-1970. The baths were recently the subject of a major renovation project.

Lyon Street used to run from just north of the baths to join Garscube Road, but all trace of it and its buildings has disappeared in redevelopment. It found some fame as the most decorated street in the UK in the First World War. It was a predominantly Irish immigrant area, but despite the strength of Irish Nationalist feeling at that time, large numbers from its closes joined the armed forces and many served with distinction and were officially rewarded for their efforts. Motives for joining up would have been varied – excitement, escaping unemployment or poorly-paid work, and in some cases apparently 'Fighting the Hun' was offered as an alternative to a spell in Duke Street Jail. Estimations of the number of medals awarded to the men of Lyon Street are as varied as the tellers of the tale. The same ambiguity applies to recollections of the memorial to the men, an icon now lost, which once graced a local pub – or was shuttled between various pubs – in North Woodside. Some say it was a properly carved war memorial, others that it was a simple wooden plaque, hand-painted. Whatever the truth of the story, the plaque has – with Lyon Street – vanished from the face of the earth.

On the other, western, side of St George's Road are extensive housing developments from the 1960s in the then-fashionable high-rise mode. Re-clad in the '80s, these are certainly striking, but at the moment the fate of such blocks is uncertain. My personal feeling is that there is too great a rush to demolish the high-rises (as there was with the tenements) rather than to re-develop, and that we may live again to regret such excessive thoughtless destruction. If the dominant form of middle-class urban housing is now the high-rise block, why isn't it – if suitably funded and renovated – an option for social housing? Why not ask those who live there? People have had enough of planners knowing best.

These two housing developments are welded together by St George's Road, which is a pleasing and interesting street. Most of the tenements are gone; many replaced by the new style of tenement buildings from the 80s onwards, but a couple of older ones remain. The most interesting is the housing block of the former Fire Station, a dwelling with large carved sandstone reliefs of the tools of the fireman's trade on the front, showing pride in both the job and the building. One of the attractions a century ago of the fireman's job was the good housing offered with it – as well as good wages and conditions – and a pension! Next to this is St George's in the Fields, the last of Woodside's trio of fine ecclesiastical buildings. Built in 1885 by H & D Barclay, this is one of Glasgow's best High Victorian churches, with its Ionic portico and sculptured tympanum of Christ's loaves and fishes miracle by William Rhind. Certainly in Woodside, when times were hard, a repeat of that miracle would have been most welcome to its inhabitants. The church is now a private housing development.

This exploration does not exhaust the riches of this street, which extend far beyond what many would be surprised to find in such a little known or visited *locale*. A little southward we come to a neat, isolated villa, complete with its own cobbled carriage-way and stable, the latter now a garage. This was one of a trio built in the 1830s as country houses for Glasgow businessmen, when the area was still a vista of open fields. The other villas are long since gone, but this jewel has survived, and is even still used as housing. About 100 yards further on we come to Clarendon Place, surely one of Glasgow's finest 'tenements' – though the word hardly applies to this colonnaded monument to architectural ambition. What on earth is this doing here? At the time of its construction in the late 1830s, this building was designed to be one of the two such constructions flanking the entrance to Great Western Road, one of Europe's Grand Boulevards, whose story has been told in Gordon Urquhart's magnificent book *Along Great Western Road* (2000). As industry swamped the surrounding area, this plan was abandoned, leaving Clarendon Place in increasingly un-splendid isolation, surrounded by industrial and slum developments. Thankfully it survived and is restored as an imposing sentinel at the Cross.

Before we come to the Cross, however, there is much more to see. In 1905, Andrew Carnegie gave Glasgow a large grant for books on the condition that the Corporation built the libraries to house them. The architect JH Rhind (no relation of the sculptor mentioned above) won the coveted contract and built six fine buildings to house the volumes, one of which is the Woodside Library. It shares the features of the other buildings Rhind created, with a huge cupola allowing for light penetration, and symbolic sculptures representing 'Learning' outside. The Library also contains an illuminating display about the history of the Woodside area which is well worth looking at. One thing you can't look at any more – though there is material about it in the library exhibition – is the once-adjacent West End Playhouse, now demolished and replaced by modern flats. This was Woodside's Music Hall, with an extravagant Baroque interior, and French Second Empire exterior – architecturally eclectic as many such buildings were. Latterly it was operated as the Metropole Theatre by the late well-loved comedian and actor Jimmy Logan, before finally closing its doors in the 1970s.

The Cross has another focal point in the impressive statue of *St George and the Dragon,* executed by Glasgow's best civic sculptors in the Victorian era, J & G Mossman Ltd. It originally stood atop the local Co-operative buildings which lay across the road, but demolition of the building led to the statue's relocation to this small, landscaped area. The symbolism of the statue is now lost on most people, representing as it does the St George of co-operation overcoming the capitalist dragon of competition.

The dreaded 'Maryhill' may have been mentioned above, but we

Metropole Poster
An advertising poster from the 1970s for a *Metropole* performance featuring the local actor John Cairney and the ever popular subject of Rabbie Burns.

are still in Woodside, and any doubters should take a short walk to Glenfarg Street, where the City Council's Woodside Halls still function as a social centre. It is a diminutive building in red brick with stone dressing in a popular 1920s style that was dubbed 'Wrenaissance'. Opposite is another very tall red and yellow brick building, now converted to housing, in a similar architectural style which dates from the same period. This was built by the City Bakeries, and was known for its high-quality products. Unlike most smallish employers here, the bakery recognised trade unions and was famed for its unusually hygienic working conditions and reasonable pay. One former employee recalls how

> the City Bakeries had the reputation for being a good employer to work for, because wages and conditions were good for those days. I got £3 a week. The management arranged social events, theatre evenings and a craft class. The factory was always clean and we were supplied with decent uniforms.

This information comes from a collection of reminiscences which was put together in the 1980s, as Woodside's remaining industry almost vanished, entitled *Working Lives in Woodside and North Kelvin 1900–1960*. Almost alone in being esteemed so highly, the bakery receives plaudits from its workers, most of whom mention low pay, unhealthy and dangerous work and the constant threat of dismissal as the norm of their working experience elsewhere. The volume paints a picture of living and working in the Woodside area with an authenticity that it would be impossible for me to convey, and inappropriate to plagiarise. The booklet can be consulted in Glasgow's Mitchell Library, as can a companion volume, *Life in the Woodside Tenements*, which I'm sure will cure anyone of misplaced nostalgia for slum housing. The story of people queuing in the morning before going to work at the few public toilets in the area, as their own were malfunctioning, is one that sticks particularly in my mind.

Continuing north along Maryhill Road, at Hopehill Road one is given the opportunity (if not taken earlier) to go and visit St Columba's RC Church, but before doing so, it is a worthwhile experience to make a short stop at the Stockline Memorial Garden. Most of Woodside's industry has disappeared, but some remained in the area, amongst the warehouses and shops which largely replaced manufacturing. In 2005 nine workers were killed at the Stockline Plastics factory here in a massive explosion. Subsequent investigations found the owners guilty of breaches of health and safety regulations, and they were fined £400,000. Whether or not one thinks that this is a suitable sum for nine lives, a visit to the memorial garden is a moving experience, and possibly a fitting place to end a visit to an area well worth investigating.

The *Woodside Bar* lies just across the road. Look up and you will see an owl on its roof. A pint here may refresh you after your walk – just avoid the word 'Maryhill' and you will be made welcome! When you come back out, the owl will still be there; the wise old stone bird is another of Woodside's icons. We hear nowadays about the Street Museum, about trying to take examples of our heritage out of their glass cages and into the public domain. For those with eyes to see, and who know where and how to look, the monuments and icons of the past are out there already and around us every day, as this stroll round the *quartier oublie* of North Woodside shows.

CHAPTER EIGHT

The Maryhill Panels: Stephen Adam's Stained Glass Workers

THE STAINED GLASS revival in the Victorian period was to a great extent religiously inspired. This corresponded with the religious revival then occurring more generally in Scotland, as the bourgeoisie sought to revive Christian values in the context of what they saw as an increasingly secular working class. No other Victorian city embraced stained glass quite as Glasgow did. Michael Donnelly points this out in *Scotland's Stained Glass* (1997), in which he describes Glasgow as the 'Second City of Empire and First City of Glass'. Once Presbyterian opposition to the art form was overcome, the church-building programmes of the Free Kirk and the Kirk of Scotland after the Disruption of 1843 created much custom for the glass industry. As time passed, other Victorian public buildings such as courts and town halls were deemed incomplete without stained glass, and increasingly the rich owners of urban villas commissioned bespoke panels as features for their own homes.

It would be rather churlish to complain that stained glass artists ignored the theme of labour for that of religion, when church commissions were, after all, their main bread and butter. When the stained glass artists' church work does show fishermen or other workers, these are generally clothed in biblical styles. By contrast, medieval stained glass artists were bolder, often showing their workers in then-contemporary clothing, utilising then-contemporary machinery. But there is an exception to this rule – Stephen Adam's Stained Glass Workers, 20 stained such panels executed for Maryhill Burgh Halls in 1878. These panels show the trades of Maryhill, and were based on intensive studies of working men and women in their

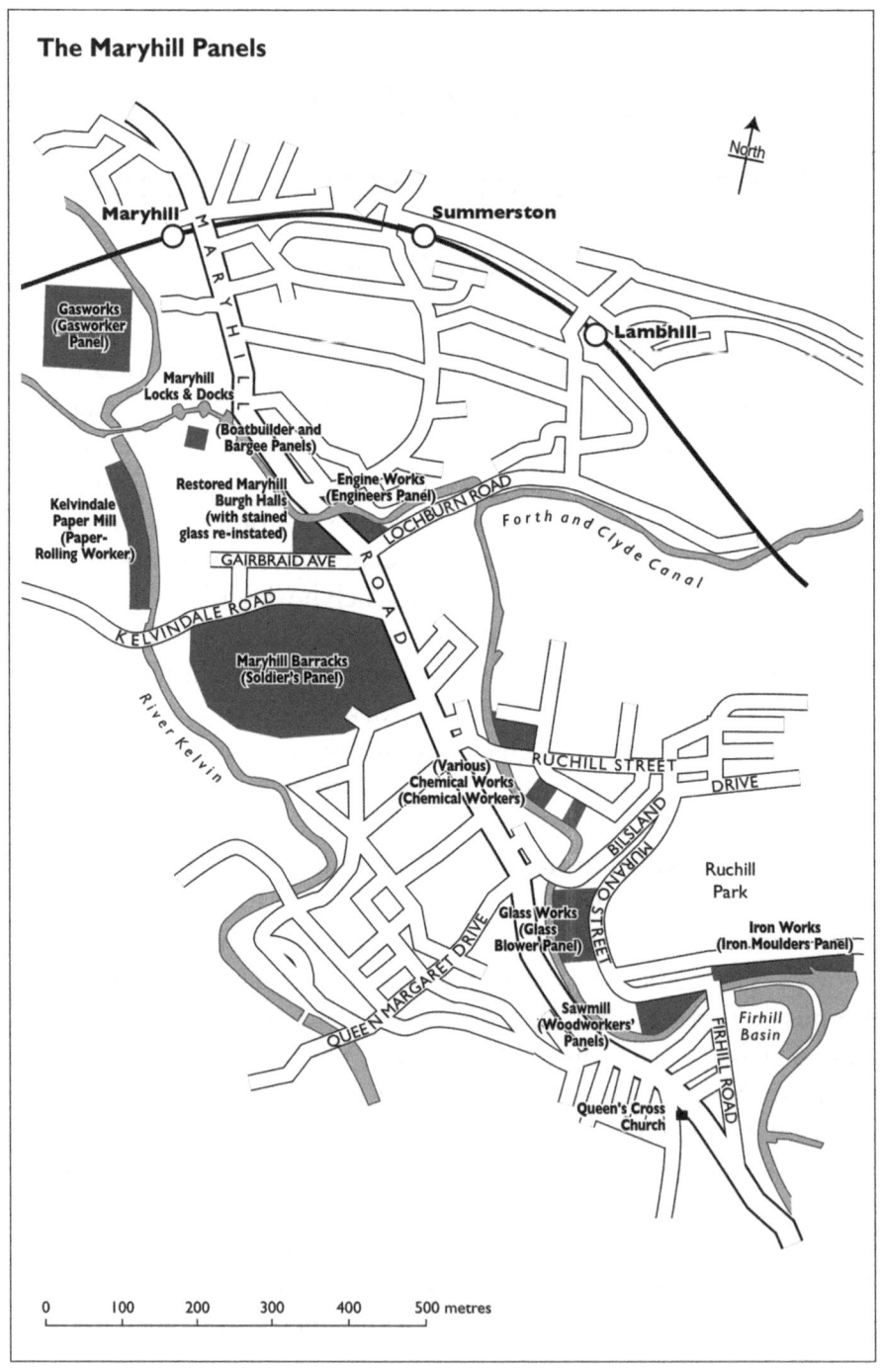

industrial situations, showing in great detail their machinery, production techniques, tools and clothing, down to a patch on one knee of a pair of trousers. Executed with great sympathy as well as accuracy, the Maryhill panels represent one of the largest and most realistic collection of portraits of labour in two centuries. This, apart from their intrinsic artistic merit, makes them of world-historic importance.

In the chapter 'Maryhill Unlocked' of my book *This City Now* (2005), I included what little information – a mere two paragraphs – I had at that time about their provenance, and also reproduced some examples of the glass panels. After involvement with the restoration of the now re-opened Burgh Halls, I am in a better position to give the interested reader a more detailed account of Adam and of the significance of his depictions of industrial labour in the Maryhill commission.

Stephen Adam was not a Glaswegian, though he carried out his business in the city. He was born near Edinburgh in 1847 and educated at Canonmills School, where he and Robert Louis Stevenson were classmates. In 1862 Adam was apprenticed to James Ballantine of Edinburgh, at that time Scotland's leading firm working in stained glass and responsible for heading the revival in the craft after centuries of Presbyterian disapproval. Adam attended Glasgow School of Art (then called the Haldane Academy) from 1865 and was awarded a silver medal for the best stained glass panel that year. In the later 1860s he was working with Alexander 'Greek' Thomson on stained glass for Holmwood House (now owned by the National Trust for Scotland) and Queen's Park Church, both in Glasgow. This connection survived Thomson's death and in 1890 Adam produced a *Cleopatra* door panel for Thomson-designed Pollokshields villa *The Knowe,* reminding us that Thomson was as much Egyptian as Greek.

In the last quarter of the 19th century, there were 30 separate stained glass workshops in the city, employing several hundred craftsmen as well as over 100 designers. Adam set up his own stained glass firm in 1870, and after a couple of partnerships was joined in the firm by his son, and the company produced possibly the best stained glass in Scotland for the next four decades, until Stephen

Adam Snr's death in 1910. The studio was originally located on St Vincent Street, later moving to Bath Street, and Adam himself lived on West George Street, at the heart of the vibrant Glasgow artistic scene of those years.

It must have been refreshing for Stephen Adam to work on the Maryhill commission, though sadly it has not been possible to locate the records of his firm which might have left us his sketches and thoughts as he worked on the project. There is a hint in a short work published by him in 1877, based on a public lecture he gave, that he welcomed an alternative to religious themes. *Stained Glass: its History and Development* criticised the Gothic Revival and its effect on stained glass, adding that 'these deformities are manufactured and catalogued principally in London; and the country is overrun with stock saints and evangelists of all sizes, at per foot prices'.

For much of the rest of his career Adam's bread and butter were church windows, characterised by examples of such 'stock saints and evangelists'. Pollokshields Parish Church, Bearsden New Kilpatrick Church and many others saw his talents displayed. In addition, his firm executed work in mansions such as that of the threadmaster Thomas Coats of Ferguslie, of the ironmaster Walter Macfarlane at 22 Park Circus (formerly the Glasgow Registry Office), and in the head offices of the Clyde Navigation Trust on the Broomielaw.

We cannot deal with the above-mentioned works here, and Adam awaits his biographer. Instead we will look in detail at the panels produced for Maryhill, which was still an independent burgh in the 1870s. These works are astounding, and would at first sight – despite sharing some of the Pre-Raphaelite touches of the artistic period – correspond more to the Socialist Realist School than that of the Gothic Revival, and are more like the Stakhanovites of Soviet Russian art than the stained glass saints beloved of Victorian Scotland. Sympathetic portrayals of *The Glassworker, The Boat Builder, The Chemical Worker, The Sawmill Worker* and many others graced the windows of Maryhill Burgh Halls for almost a century from 1878. The Halls were closed shortly after the 1991 centenary of the annexation of Maryhill by Glasgow, but even before that the panels were considered to be in danger, removed in the 1960s and held for safe keeping first in the People's Palace and then in the basement of the Burrell Collection.

Adam's panels depict working men and women, dressed in working clothes, engaged about their daily occupations. Adam must have spent much time in Maryhill's factories, as his depiction of not only the clothing of the workmen, but also of their machinery and tools, is remarkably detailed and accurate. Michael Donnelly comments in *Scotland's Stained Glass* (1997) of the set as a whole that the 'accuracy of the detail leaves little doubt that the preliminary sketches for these panels were done in the field... Both the subject matter of the scheme and its treatment are unique'. He adds that the 'kind of industrial setting' of the panels was what most artists of the time later 'avoided like the plague'. Why the good burghers of Maryhill chose Adam and his industrial themes with which to decorate their Halls we cannot be sure. The Burgh Council of the time was composed of the fairly small-scale capitalists of Maryhill and it is difficult to see artistic merit being their main concern. Whatever their motivation, it is interesting that Adam was still chasing up the council for payment of the balance for the stained glass panels in 1881!

Sadly, the Burgh Council records for the years 1875–80, which might have helped us, are now missing from Glasgow's Mitchell Library, but possibly the motivation for the commission was the fact that, unlike other Glasgow industrial districts such as Govan (largely based on shipbuilding) and Springburn (overwhelmingly dominated by locomotive production), Maryhill had a varied industrial base, focussed on the Forth and Clyde canal. Its councillors might well have wished to have this reflected, indeed to have recorded the processes that took place in some of their very own workshops. The variety of Maryhill's industries provided a fortuitous variety of subject matter for the panels, and indeed it is interesting to speculate that the local employers might have perceived them as a form of advertising for their businesses, displayed in the most important place in the burgh.

Provost Robertson opened the new Halls, which cost £8,500 to build, on 26 April 1878. A previous occupant of the burgh office was Provost Swan in 1856, and he provides some evidence for the theory of the panels as a form of advertising. He was from the family which owned the canal boatyard at Kelvin Dock, depicted in a panel entitled *The Boat Builder*. The worker shown is a ship's carpenter with his plane and shaping adze. Kelvin Dock, dating from the 1790s, was run as a boatyard by Swan & Co. in the 1850s and remained open for production until the 1920s. The boatyard built ironclad puffers, but the vessel shown is a wooden canal barge with a swan motif. Another industrial concern was the nearby factory producing zinc, also owned by Swan, which is represented in the panel *The Spelter Workers*. The factory was a highly polluting concern and could have been one of the reasons why Swan moved from his mansion *Colina*, which lay near the Kelvin Dock, to suburban Maryhill Park. The brick wall of the former spelter works is still partly visible beside the Kelvin Dock.

Further evidence for the argument that the panels were intended as adverts is that at least one other councillor, Mr Shaw, a partner in Shaw and MacInnes' Ironworks, seems to have had his company advertised in the Burgh Halls. Though there were many ironworks in Maryhill the largest and longest lasting concern – closing only in the early 21st century – was this one, which lay by the bascule bridge on the Firhill basin. *The Ironmoulders* panel shows the riveted foundry, the bars of pig iron and the workmen – without any protective clothing, and this was a dangerous job! – using their ladles to pour molten metal into the pig moulds.

It is possible to suggest other firm or likely locations for many of the Adam stained glass panels by looking at the evidence provided by industrial archaeology. John R Hume's *The Industrial Archaeology of Glasgow* (1973) is still an extremely useful document 40 years after its initial publication, and other sources such as old ordnance survey and other maps evince how such works as *The Gas Worker* could clearly refer to the Dawsholm Gasworks, opened in 1872 and owned by Glasgow Corporation. Glasgow's provision

The Canal Bridge
The exterior of Shaw and MacInnnes' ironworks on the canal at Firhill, the most likely inspiration for Adam's panel 'The Ironworkers'. (J. Brown, 1923).

of services like these was used as an argument for the city's annexation of Maryhill in 1891. The panel not only shows the workman in his industrial clothing but also the process of production from coke oven to gas retort to storage tank, the latter detailed down to the iron rivets. The workman used as a model for this panel quite possibly took part in the gas workers' strikes in the 1880s, which lead to the New Unionism amongst unskilled and semi-skilled workers of that decade. The gas works was demolished in 1968.

Other panels can be similarly pinpointed. *The Railway Workers* shows a station in Maryhill, and, as Maryhill Central was not built until 1896, long after the panel was executed, this example must show Maryhill Park Station, built in 1856 for the Glasgow, Dumbarton and Helensburgh Railway. Closed in the 1960s, this station was reopened in the 1990s; imagine how its appearance would benefit from a large-scale reproduction of this image. The panel shows that the station was manned by a railway porter, had a covered roof (both no more) and in addition was a parcel station, the platform littered with goods bound for various locations.

Maryhill had two large-scale glass works, both in Murano Street, which was named after the Murano Glass works in Venice. The titular *Glassworker* is shown with a wide variety of blown glass products. The Caledonia Glass Bottle Works, under its owners Gibson & Scott, had been operating since 1874, and it seems likely that these are the works captured in the stained glass panel. The Glasgow Glass Works were also established on the canal banks in 1874, but produced rolled plate glass and are therefore unlikely to be the inspiration. Both works had closed by 1973. This panel features one of the few workers without a beard and the reason appears to be that he is a mere boy. Child labour, especially in a part-time work/part-time schooling form, was still common in the 1870s.

Possibly the most interesting panels are those depicting women textile workers, such as *The Bleachers* and *The Calico Printers*. Maryhill in the 1870s still had a calico printworks, established back in the 1830s. Barr's Kelvindale Works had seen a violent strike in 1834 when the factory was occupied by the military and a striking workman George Millar was killed by a 'nab' (scab). Millar's fellow workmen erected a memorial to him in Maryhill Old Kirk Graveyard. This industry was in decline when Adam completed his panel, and the factory closed soon afterwards. Thomson's *Memories of Maryhill*, dating from 1895, describes the works as having been demolished. The fact that the bleachers are whitening the cloth in sunlight (after it would have been soaked in urine) rather than using a chemical bleaching process possibly indicates – as do some of the other panels – the technologically backward nature of Maryhill's industry at this time. On the other hand, some of the women in *The Calico Printers* panel have clogs to keep their feet dry, and the employer has provided duck-boards to keep their feet out of the water. At some point erroneously labelled *The Calico Printers*, the women are not in actual fact printing, but are fulling (shrinking) or dyeing the cloth. Another panel in somewhat poorer condition has been identified as a male worker using a calico press to print the cloth, and this was most probably executed in the latter days of the Kelvindale works.

Possible further evidence of technological backwardness is found in *The Papermaker* panel where the machinery is clearly made out of wood, which would have been cheaper than metal, and is hand-operated, not power-driven. Unlike other industries, which moved to the canal with steam power, the paper mills stayed on the River Kelvin because of their need for large amounts of water. The man in this image is either working at the Dalsholm Paper Mills, founded by William MacArthur in 1783 on Dalsholm Road near Dalsholm Bridge, or, more likely, at the Kelvindale Mills further downriver at Kelvindale Road, established at about the same time as a snuff mill and later converted to paper making. These latter works' lade and weir are still visible on the Kelvin. Dalsholm closed in the 1970s, by which time Kelvindale had also shut down.

For *The Sawmill Worker,* there is a trio of possible locations. Mac-Farlane's Ruchill Sawmills in Shuna Street was operating in 1878. The man shown might be working there, or at either the Firhill Sawmills or the Western Sawmills, both of which were located at Firhill Timber Basin, a facility built with the canal but greatly extended from 1849. Ruchill Sawmills became part of Bryant and May's match factory c.1918, while the Western Sawmills had converted to a chemical works by 1896, with the Firhill Sawmills being the last to go in 1968. More than any other panel this shows the dangerous working conditions of the time, with the workman's loose clothing and hair in clear danger of being drawn into unprotected parts of the machinery like the overhead drivebelts, the sawing machinery, and of course, the rotary saw blade itself. This panel captures with startling immediacy the myriad ways in which the worker could die or suffer great injury.

In *The Chemical Workers* the workers appear engaged in some kind of distillation process. Of the various chemical related industries in Maryhill, several would have been operative when Adam completed this panel. A likely candidate, though, is the Glasgow Lead and Colour Works of Alexander Fergusson, which dates from 1874 and was on both sides of Ruchill Street, with a wharf to the canal. The point made above about safety – or lack of it – is again evident here, as the workers wear neither hand nor, more vitally, eye protection.

The Sawmills
The exterior of Firhill sawmills on the canal fifty years after Adam depicted one of the workers in its interior. It survived another 50 years. (J. Brown, 1923).

The almost certain source for *The Engineers* would have been the Maryhill Engine Works at Lochburn Road, built in 1873 for Clarkson Brothers, later Clarkson & Becket. It is possible that it is one of the brothers who is seen explaining to the workman the requirements of the latest job. These works produced steam engines, and careful analysis of the drawing sheet reveals a small steam engine to be built, in all likelihood for a canal barge. The workman is again in corduroy *breeks* – denim dungarees were still a decade or two away – and like many others in the panels wears not a *bunnet* or cloth cap, but a Tam o' Shanter headpiece. The building which housed this factory is still standing, to my knowledge the only one so doing in the entire set of panels, and remarkably it still houses a small engineering works.

The historical information contained in these panels is extensive and revealing. How many visual examples remain, one wonders, of how scaffolding was erected in the High Victorian period? *The Bricklayers* panel shows us a couple of fellows on a scaffold. The wooden scaffolding is shown in some detail, as are the wooden ladders, and, perhaps most importantly, the rope knots, minutely delineated, holding the whole construction together. Most of Maryhill was built of stone – the tenements, the barracks, the churches and the civic buildings. On the other hand, many of the factories beside the canal were brick built, and this panel probably shows one of these being constructed.

The Soldiers reminds us that Maryhill was a military town. Just opened in 1876 when Adam devised this panel, the Maryhill Barracks were used by various regiments until eventually becoming associated with the Highland Light Infantry or HLI. The building where the two *sodjers* from the panel are shown could well be the still extant gatehouse, looking out onto the tenements on Maryhill Road, or possibly inwards to the barracks themselves. The military connection with the area ended in the early 1960s, when the barracks were closed and the Wyndford housing estate built on its grounds. The wall of the barracks still stands and carries a memorial to its history on the corner of Garrioch Road and Maryhill Road. Proposals by a well-meaning local councillor to demolish the barracks wall and 'unite the Wyndford estate with the rest of Maryhill' were greeted with horror by the locals and abandoned. Part of this reaction was motivated by heritage, and part by the desire to 'keep the folk fae the Gilshie and Gairbraid (other local estates) oot'.

Representations of workers by Adam also exist in Trinity Hall, Aberdeen, depicting 'The Trades'. However, these panels – stunning as they are – were executed in a different style from the Maryhill panels, a style which was more acceptable to Victorian taste. The Trinity Hall *Butcher*, for example, is dressed in Biblical garments and *The Weaver* in medieval ones. The Burgh Hall panels are unique, and they did not set a precedent; in bourgeois High Victorian Art industrial production is virtually invisible. Stratten's *Glasgow and its Environs* (1891), a business guide to the city, mentions much of Adam's work in the entry on his firm, but interestingly not the Maryhill commission, despite it being probably the company's largest single work.

Adam appears to have been a clubbable man, giving slide lectures in the Art Gallery to the Ecclesiological Society and being a member of both the Glasgow Philosophical Society and the Society of Literature and Arts. His photograph in the 1896 short pamphlet *Truth in Decorative Art* shows a well-dressed, if slightly bohemian, character. His son, Stephen, was an associate of Charles Rennie Macintosh and worked on various Glasgow tearooms including Pettigrew and Stephens' in Sauchiehall Street. He also did the stained glass windows for the Imperial Bar in Howard Street which are still *in situ*. When his stained glass studio was unsuccessful, Stephen Adam Jr. emigrated to the USA, where he worked on film sets in Hollywood, and he died there in 1960.

Stephen Adam
A photograph of the slightly bohemian-looking Stephen Adam, rather later than when he executed the Maryhill panels.

There have been various schemes envisaged for the regeneration of Maryhill and of the canal (which has recently been reopened to navigation after being closed for 50 years). New housing has been built along the canal banks where the workplaces Adam depicted formerly stood, and there are ideas for transforming the wonderful Maryhill Locks and Kelvin Dock, with its associated Kelvin Aqueduct (finished by Whitworth in 1790 and a scheduled Ancient Monument), into a focal point for leisure industries on the canal. Amongst these plans, regenerating the Burgh Halls was central. The building (with associated police and fire stations, and swimming pool) had been left to decay after closure two decades ago, but the restoration of the former swimming pool to its original function has now been undertaken by the Glasgow City Council, and a Trust was established to raise funds for the restoration of the Burgh Halls for use in various community and business purposes. After seven years of work, planning and fundraising, the Burgh Halls were re-opened in April 2012.

Fifty years ago, a local Maryhill working man and political activist moved mountains to get the stained glass panels taken into the care of the People's Palace. He was told by all and sundry 'no-one is interested', but his persistence paid off. Too ill to attend the official re-opening of the Halls in 2012, Stewart Watson, a real working class hero, was taken on a personal tour of the building just weeks before his death, and was able to see the panels back in place after 50 years. Ten of Stephen Adam's stained glass panels are in the halls on public display and the other ten will be rotated with them on a semi-permanent loan basis from the city council. The Halls also have excellent pamphlets, available for visitors, on both the stained glass itself and on the heritage of Maryhill. Before you go and see the Dali at Kelvingrove, visit Adam's stained glass panels of his working class heroes.

NOTE: an excellent free, lavishly illustrated 24-page pamphlet has been published on the *Historic Stained Glass Windows* by Maryhill Burgh Halls Trust, which has also produced three, free *Maryhill Walking Trail* brochures giving various options for walks round the sites of the former industries and other points of interest in Maryhill. Details can be found at:

www.maryhillburghhalls.org.uk   info@mbht.org.uk
tel 0845 860 1856.

Do remember to make a donation to the work of the Trust, and to visit the café, where postcard reproductions of the stained glass panels are available for sale.

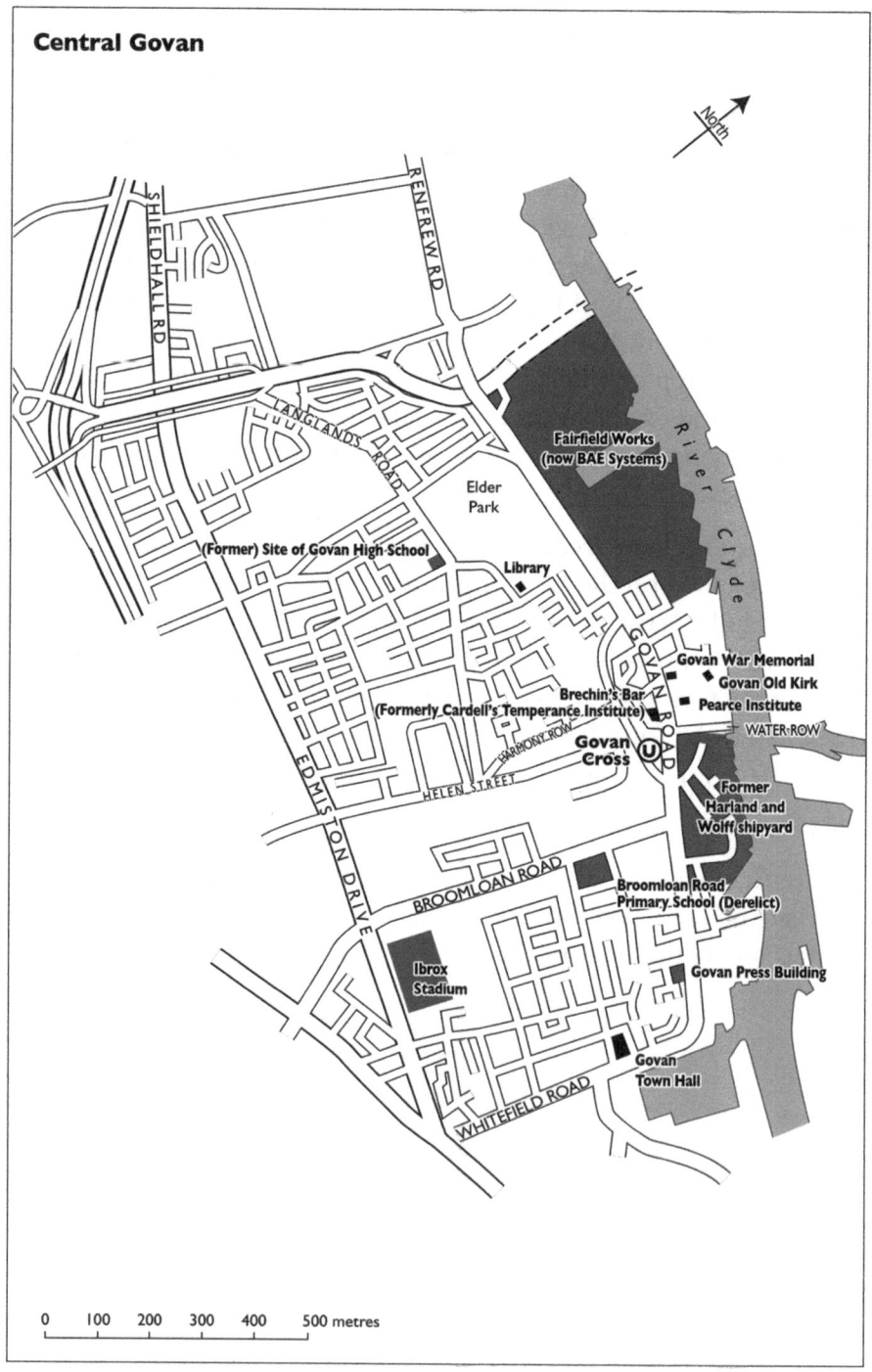

CHAPTER NINE

The Rise and Fall of the Old Govan Club: 1914–39

THE RICHNESS OF civil society in the period preceding World War Two is easily forgotten in today's more atomised community. In the absence of the ubiquitous availability of packaged mass entertainment, social, sporting and political organisations in the earlier part of last century had membership levels and attendance at their meetings and other gatherings that would today seem incredible. Govan (which today lies within Glasgow city on the south bank of the River Clyde but which existed pre-1912 as an independent burgh) was a place of active social culture. Its range of sporting clubs, choirs, political and church organisations was extensive, as a glance at the *Govan Directory* (c.1914) will confirm. Many social clubs and societies survived long past that date, and amongst these the Old Govan Club was surely one of the more historically interesting. Established to collect and disseminate information on the history of Govan, its own history and activities mirror in many ways Govan's identity crisis in the early 20th century, and the district's post-World War One economic difficulties. As the former 'Capital of World Shipbuilding' undergoes yet another massive redevelopment today – and experiences more identity issues – it is pertinent to recall the role the Old Govan Club played in its past.

The 1911 census showed that the then independent burgh of Govan was the 5th largest settlement in Scotland, after the four main cities, and with almost 100,000 people it had many more inhabitants than the next most populous town, which was Paisley. Most of the burgh's growth had taken place in the previous half-century since 1861, at which date its population had been nearer to 10,000. With a 2,000-year history going back to the Kingdom of Strathclyde and beyond, Govan had an intense civic pride and sense of identity, despite the vast majority of its population in around 1900 being first-generation immigrants and their offspring. Its anti-annexationist battles were testimony to this.

For much of the 19th century, Glasgow tried – and failed – to annex Govan. Initially these attempts were beaten back by the local Burgh Council, which in 1901 opened the huge Govan Town Hall as a statement of its independent intent. This fabulous Beaux Arts palace, with its busts of provosts and councilors and a 2,000 seat theatre, testified to the wealth of the burgh at that time. The large sandstone relief on the front of the Town Hall of the Govan coat of arms (a ship's carpenter and a ship's engineer) reflected pride in the taproot of this wealth. The council was supported in the fight against annexation by the highly successful local newspaper, the *Govan Press*, which was established by printer and book publisher John Cossar in 1883. In the 1900s the main reporter on the *Govan Press* was TCF Brotchie. Like Stephen Adam, Brotchie was an Edinburgh man who had left the *Evening News* in the capital to come and work for the *Govan Press*. Despite his east-coast origins, Brotchie became Govan's leading patriot, and in 1905 – four years after the official opening of the Town Hall – the *Govan Press* published Brotchie's *History of Govan*. The fruit of much research and enthusiasm, Brotchie's book was written by a journalist rather than an academic, and, though a great read, many of its historical arguments require substantial qualification. For example, Brotchie took the existence of Viking-influenced hogback gravestones in Govan as evidence of a Viking settlement, which was not the case. As well as highlighting the collection of more than 30 early Christian incised stones in the graveyard of Govan Old Kirk, Brotchie tracked Govan's claims to fame through its period as a weaving centre to its later industrial greatness, and the result was a polemic against annexation, arguing that Govan could, and should, maintain its independence against its mighty, expansionist neighbour. His *History of Govan* thundered that

> keen though the former fights were, Glasgow will find that her opponent is prepared for a more prolonged struggle than any of the former battles. Financially, Govan today is thoroughly sound. She can afford a fight. Can the same be applied to the city?

Although Brotchie's book was a commercial success, the campaign against annexation ultimately failed, and in 1912, in the last of Glasgow's great boundary expansions, Govan and several other areas were absorbed into the city. Whither Govan?

Brotchie
The genial and clubbable Govan patriot and historian – despite having come from Edinburgh and later having taking Glasgow's shilling.

Having failed in the fight to maintain Govan's independence, Brotchie was determined to retain its traditions, and he was the inspiration behind the formation of the Old Govan Club, founded two years after Govan had become wards 27, 28, 29 and 30 of Glasgow. Brotchie also became the editor of the club's *Transactions*. Ironically, the inspiration for the new club came from across the Clyde, provided by the Old Glasgow Club which had been formed in 1900 and is still operating today. Brotchie was a member of this 'parent' club and had given lectures on Govan there. His fears that Govan's identity would be lost, submerged in that of Glasgow and Glasgow-wide organisations, may not have been unfounded. When I spoke in 2007 to the Old Glasgow Club on *The Glories of Govan,* it was their first lecture on that subject since those by Brotchie a century before.

John Strang's wonderful book *Glasgow and its Clubs* (1856) describes the club-organised social gatherings in the city in pre-Victorian and early Victorian times. Though they had an intellectual input, the main function of these clubs was a social one, especially that of eating and, more especially, drinking. The Partick Duck Club, for example, was not a philosophical debating society, but a convivial outfit dedicated to feasting and washing down copious quantities of roast bird with lashings of port. By later Victorian and Edwardian times, clubs had a more serious import. Generally they were seen as 'improving' organisations, where informative lectures replaced an extensive bill of gastronomic fare, and tea and biscuits replaced alcohol. The Old Govan Club held its founding meeting in the Cardell Temperance Halls on 29 April 1914, and for a long time afterwards the club met in the Christian Institute, indicating that its concern was instruction rather than self-indulgence.

The instruction the members of the club received was to be in the history and traditions of their burgh. The first rule was that 'The Club shall have for its objects the study and discussion of matters relating to local history'. As the first edition of the *Transactions* (also published by Cossar's *Govan Press*) stated,

> we love our native town and our native village. How can we love the British Empire, which we have not seen, if we love not the town we have seen?

This was written when Britain was already at war, and indeed the first public meeting did not take place until November 1914, by which time hostilities were well underway. Despite the difficulties posed by the war, the club enrolled 175 members by the end of its first year, and around 90 per cent of these were from within the pre-1912 boundaries of the burgh, according to the list of members and their residences printed in the first issue of the *Transactions*. There was a low subscription rate of 2/6d, and the club declared itself non-partisan in Rule 18, which stated that 'all political, partisan and sectarian subjects and discussions thereon are absolutely debarred at meetings of the Club'. Except for its being (fairly usually for the times) male only, the Club thus aimed at inclusivity in its membership. But there were unspoken assumptions underlying the Club, apparently not questioned by its members. Its meeting places had associations with temperance, with Christianity (or at least with its Protestant variant) and support for the Empire was so taken for granted that its mention, above, was not assumed to be any way political. One might expect, therefore, that its membership was composed of people like Brotchie, who were middle class. Certainly Govan's Catholic minority would not have felt comfortable in the

Club, nor probably would non-temperance folk (Govan's alcohol problem at this time was endemic), nor indeed might the growing number of those unconnected with any organised religion, but membership of the Old Govan Club was much wider than a circle of middle class protestant Unionists.

Govan was an overwhelmingly working class area in 1914, with around 80 per cent of the population living in one-('single end') or two-('room and kitchen') roomed tenements, and it was economically dominated by work in the shipyards, three of which – Stephens', Fairfield's, and Harland and Wolff – employed almost 15,000 men between them. But the yards also gave work to clerks, foremen and draughtsmen, and there was a middle class of shopkeepers, small businessmen and professionals in the burgh. If only 20 per cent of the population were middle class, that's still almost 20,000 people in 1914!

Certainly, looking at the office bearers and the speakers of the club, especially early in its existence, it would appear to have been

Club's 'At Home' (Brotchie)
Initially 'Old Govan' was represented by pre-industrial Govan, as this illustration with its old weavers' cottages shows.

dominated by Govan's middle class – for example the publisher Cossar, who was a long-time member. Of the speakers who can be identified in the early days, there is a preponderance of educated professionals such as teachers, ministers (although no priests), doctors and the librarian of the Elder Park library in the burgh. However, it would be wrong to see the club as only the preserve of Govan's middle class.

Many of the streets where the members are listed as living (in the initially annual *Transactions*) were entirely or predominantly working class, such as Water Row and Helen Street. A Mr J Purdie (who had been a founder member of the Club) was given Life Membership in 1921 with the revealing comment that

> he was a Labour leader when workers, as a rule, looked upon anyone who espoused their cause, as one who had 'a bee in their bonnet', while employers looked upon him with intense dislike and treated him hotly.
>
> *Transactions* III, 2

In 1931, the Club's President, Donald Macleod, gave his account of 'The "Black Squad" in Former Days', recalling his shipyard experiences in late Victorian times, and in passing referred to another Club member, John Hill, who had been Secretary of the Boilermakers' Society, a trade union with 100,000 members nationally. The same issue of the *Transactions* (Vol. V, 1.) features the obituary of a William Robertson, who had been a ship's carpenter, an active trade unionist, a Kirk elder and a supporter of the YMCA. William Lawson was of a similar mould, and his obituary in 1938 noted that he was an activist in the Amalgamated Society of Woodworkers, and later Chairman of the Clyde Federation of Shipbuilding and Engineering Unions. He was also a Congregationalist, a Rechabite and a supporter of the Band of Hope. He was further a former President of the Old Govan Club. You wonder how he found the time.

It is clear that a number of the 'respectable' working classes – skilled, trade unionist and church-going – were interested enough in the Club to join it and to play an active part in its activities. After the War this was more often the case as the middle classes began their exit from Govan, no longer the boom town it had been before the conflict. Examination of the club's membership lists from 1920 shows a steady increase in the number of members who resided outside Govan's boundaries. From a record high of 250 members that year, 61 were from outside Govan, constituting almost 25 per cent of its membership, compared with nearer to ten per cent in 1914. Some of these would be accounted for by workers moving to the new council housing estates peripheral to Govan, such as Craigton, but most of these emigrés were middle-class people moving out and moving on. By 1938 the Club was down to 120 members, 45 of whom lived outside Govan, i.e. over 35 per cent of their membership. Cossar, for example, who had first lived 'above the shop' (in the tenement which also housed the *Govan Press* office) in Govan Road, later moved to what was then perceived to be the genteel area of Ibrox (just inside Govan), and finally to posh Bellahouston (on the other side of the tracks, literally, being separated from Govan by the railway). Even Brotchie no longer lived in his original address in Ibrox, as the club increasingly became the reserve of the old and middle-class exiles.

Despite the difficulties of the Great War, no-one foresaw such a situation when the club was founded in 1914, just as none foresaw the inter-war collapse in shipbuilding demand. Govan boomed with naval reconstruction till 1923. These post-war years were the halcyon days of the organisation. Indeed, at the AGM in 1921 it was reported that 'The Club has every reason to be satisfied with its progress'. Membership had reached 250, and women had been admitted after Dr John Macfadyen argued the previous year that 'ladies were being admitted to almost every sphere and he did not see why they should not be admitted to membership of the Club'.

As well as talks at their meetings and publication of their *Transactions,* the Club played a prominent role in the social life of Govan in this post-war period, organising concerts with local brass and pipe bands, recitations of verse by former Govan poets, and Halloween parties, where it was proudly announced that a large number of old and young folks gathered to 'haud Halloween' as it was in the days when the oldest present were the age of the youngest.

The main achievement of the Club was undoubtedly the re-establishment of the Govan Fair, an annual event which continues to this day.

The story of the Govan Fair would take a chapter in itself. Originally a medieval trade fair, it was first held in its modern form by the Govan weavers in 1756, and was continued until 1881 when the last Govan weaver died. One of the oldest fairs in Scotland, with its own rituals (such as the carrying of a sheep's head on a pole at its front), it had been discontinued for four decades when in 1920 the Old Govan Club stepped in and engaged the support of Govan MP Neil MacLean for its re-instatement. The new fair moved with the times. The Club accepted at its AGM in 1921 that it was hoped that the first Friday in June might be re-established as an 'anniversary of olden times in a modern fashion to the present generation'.

Instead of a weaver (there were, after all, none left) the 'sheep's heid' was now carried by a ship's carpenter from the Fairfield yard. This yard still exists, and still provides a pole bearer for the Fair every year. Though the Govan Weavers' Society still continued (and still does) as a Friendly Society, and though it supported the re-establishment of the Fair, no attempt was made at a pseudo-heritage revival, no recreation of the old weavers' parade. Instead of mocking the past, the parade consisted of representatives of contemporary Govan; the Govan Silver Band, the Boys Brigade Pipe Band, the Salvation Army Band, the Kinning Park Co-operative Band and the Boilermakers Band. Twenty thousand people turned out in Elder Park for the first parade. But following these successes the Club began to struggle.

The 1930s arrived almost a decade early in Govan. The post-war reconstruction boom was soon over, and this slump in demand hit British shipbuilding severely. By 1923 there was mass unemployment as the yards contracted. At the AGM of the club it was noted that Govan was 'experiencing a period of unemployment greater than has ever been known in this district', and that there had been a decline in attendance at events and in membership. It was specifically noted that many members of the Club were now unemployed, again indicating that it had a sizeable working-class component, since industrial employers at that time generally retained their salaried staff in recessions. These issues were captured and reflected upon in the main talk that year by Dr HE Jones, who in his 'Old Govan Scenes' (*Transactions* 1, 3 1922–23) recalled the recession of the 1880s:

> Employment was scarce then as now, and people were badly fed. He told how they were thrilled one morning to hear that a man had been found dead in the yard, and his breakfast piece was found to consist of two slices of turnip.

Most people were used to economic slumps, and expected this one to pass, but with minor ups and downs, the yards continued to struggle badly until the outbreak of World War Two, and the main yard, Fairfield's, went bankrupt in 1935. Between the Wars Govan's population reduced by almost 40 per cent, which works out at about 2,000 people a year leaving on average. It would have been surprising if the Club had not been greatly affected. Year on year, shrinking membership was noted, as was nonpayment of subscriptions and declining attendance at social events and meetings. Whilst bewailing these trends, Club officials were clear as to the cause, poignantly recorded at the AGM in April 1934:

> The Old Govan Club was formed to perpetuate the memories of the 'good old days', and it has done so, but it should be recorded that frequently during its earlier days it was remarked that, while it was a pleasing pastime to recall the 'good old days', few desired to return to them. Times have changed however, and a return to the 'good old days' when work was plentiful, would be welcome indeed.

Indeed, of great interest is how the idea of 'Old Govan' itself changed. In the first decade or so of the Club, Old Govan was largely (though not exclusively) seen as pre-industrial Govan, from the vantage point of a community undergoing unprecedented expansion as a 'new' burgh. Brotchie submitted regular drawings to the *Transactions* at this time, and their slightly 'Olde Worlde' flavour reflects this view of the members' 'Govan of the Mind'.

Brotchie's Steppin Stones
This illustration, with its synthetic and inaccurate Scots, conveys well the 'Olde Worlde' flavour of some of the Club's early interests.

By the mid-1920s, more of the contributions to the *Transactions* relate to later 19th-century Govan, which from the point of view of the depressed inter-war years of the economy now began to assume the aura of Bygone Days. The above quotation captures this shift in perception very well, and it is further reflected in contributions to the *Transactions* concerning Govan's days of industrial glory, such as those entitled 'Robert Napier; A Great Shipbuilder' (3, 2), 'The Fairfield Yard in 1866' (3, 3) and 'The Silk Industry in Govan' (4, 2). This was not the fare which had dominated the *Transactions* in its first decade.

The Club, like the shipyards, struggled on till 1938, when it made a presentation to the family of now-deceased founder TCF Brotchie, and a success was noted in that his *History of Govan* had been reprinted that year. It sold out quickly, but has been out of print ever since. The Club President, Walter MacIndoe, declared sadly that 'one almost feels that Govan people have forgotten the great traditions of the old burgh'. Rather, with 50 per cent to 75 per cent unemployment in the area, a middle class leaving the burgh and a skilled working class reduced to breadline poverty, the social bases of the Old Govan Club were simply disappearing. Mooted as an organisation just before the First World War, it died just before the Second.

The quality of the papers presented to the Club varied enormously, as one would expect. It should be stressed that the Club meetings initially consisted solely of talks, not slide shows, though by the 1930s the latter were creeping in. Many of the contributions were of the 'Lang Syne' variety, consisting of local worthies (and, after the war, increasingly of ex-local worthies) recalling the Govan of their youth. While most of these were anecdotal and whimsical, nuggets are occasionally found, as in the case of James Purdie's 'Reminiscences of the Municipal and Political Life of Old Govan', which recalls the first elections held in the 1880s when Govan became a parliamentary constituency (*Transactions* IV, 1 1917).

Of great interest too is M Macleod's 'The Battle of the Standard', in *Transactions* III, 3 (1925), which recalls the intense struggle over the question of the catechism in state schools in later 19th-century Govan. MacLeod's comments reveal the extent to which the world had changed since then:

> Would it be possible in our day to arouse so much public interest and so widespread an agitation in Govan in support of any theological dogma? It is very doubtful.

Some of the articles, which were read as lectures to the presumably attentive and certainly large audiences, are the fruit of real learning and research. When the Rev Roger Kirkpatrick spoke in the 1915–1916 session on the Govan Sarcophagus, he was presenting what were then up-to-date archeological hypotheses, though we now know his belief that the stone coffin found in Govan Old Churchyard was that of St Constantine to be wrong. Another weighty contribution came from JA Brown (FSA) on 'Govan Session Records of 1651' (in *Transactions* III, 1, 1916–17), dealing with the imposition of 'Godly

Discipline' by the Kirk session in those days. Others are interesting despite having no academic pretensions, such as 'Sport in Govan in Bygone Days' by Duncan Hutchinson (*Transactions* IV, 4 1929/30), in which the incredible amount of recreational exercise taken by ordinary people, and the vast number of cycling, football and other clubs they founded, is chronicled. Many of the articles can be read by the general as well as the academic reader with profit.

Increasing numbers of contributions from 'outsiders', such as the Professor of Naval Architecture at Glasgow University and the Chief of the Glasgow Police, indicate that in the period after its first decade the Club might have been struggling for speakers and topics. This is a common problem with any society that outlaws political and religious topics in its programme, since so much is excluded from consideration, but it was not lack of topics which killed the Club, rather economic problems between the World Wars did.

Nevertheless, and in spite of this chronic hardship, Govan clearly remained the mental *habitus* of those in the Old Govan Club, as indeed it did for most of its inhabitants who then – and even now – regarded Glasgow as being on the periphery of their mental horizons. Today, despite a century of annexation by its more powerful neighbour, you can walk around Govan and hardly see an example of the fish, bell, bird and tree coat of arms of Glasgow city, but on almost every public building, including those once frequented by the members of the Old Govan Club in its quarter-century of existence, the Govan coat of arms with the ship's carpenter and the ship's engineer is still visible. Not just on the former town hall, as already stated, but also on Cardell's Temperance Institute (now a pub), on the Govan Library, on the front entrance to the Fairfield Shipyard, on the now marvelously restored Aitken Memorial Fountain at Govan Cross, and on the Great War Memorial, even though this was erected after Govan lost its independence. The iconography of the district tells you where you are, and the Club certainly played a part in keeping this local identity alive.

The final and almost total collapse of the Govan economy took place in the 1980s. The further reduction of the area's population since the 1980s has left it with around 30,000 people. Just as no major UK settlement gained population before 1914 as fast as did Govan, so nowhere – to my knowledge – has lost population faster since.

The interest which led to the formation of the Old Govan Club almost a century ago is not dead. A Govan Reminiscence Group has now been operating for 20 years in the area, and has amassed a large collection of tapes and photographs. Glasgow University recently ran a successful evening class on the history of Govan, bringing together experts on the burgh's rich and varied history, and highlighting academic research taking place into Govan's past. In 2009, Historic Scotland published its Burgh Survey *Historic Govan* by Chris Dalgleish and Stephen Driscoll, which began to redress academic neglect of the area.

While it is doubtful whether 250 people will ever again gather in Govan to listen closely to an hour's lecture on the happenings of the 17th-century Kirk Session, new ways of bringing Govan's history back to the people of the area must be explored in order that the engrossing and proud legacy of the burgh can be carried forward, and can help inform its changing future. The reprinting of Brotchie's *History of Govan* and of the *Transactions* of the Old Govan Club – perhaps making them available online – would be a useful contribution to such an aim.

Further Reading

The entire collection of the *Transactions* of the Old Govan Club is held by the Mitchell Library in Glasgow, though sadly the Elder Park Library in Govan does not have them. Both libraries have complete sets of the *Govan Press*, which faithfully reported on the meetings and activities of the Club, and copies of Brotchie's *History of Govan*, which can be read with profit – and caution. *Historic Govan* by Chris Dalgleish and Stephen Driscoll goes some small way to outlining the astonishingly rich and neglected story of the burgh's history. Govan's full history remains to be written.

CHAPTER TEN

The Heart of Govan Beats Again

THE AREA AROUND Govan Cross in Glasgow is dominated by the Pearce Institute, known to Govanites as 'the PI'. It is a magnificent, A-listed building, an eclectic mix of Scottish and Dutch Renaissance styles, with crow-step gables, oriel windows, external iron balconies, and on its roof is a sculpture of a fully-rigged sailing ship built by the workers in the local Fairfield shipyard. Designed by Robert Rowand Anderson, one of the leading Scottish architects of the time, the PI celebrated its centenary in 2006. William Pearce – whose name the building bears – was chairman and owner of the Fairfield yard in Govan from 1869 until 1885 after becoming a partner in the firm, then owned by John Elder, in the 1860s. Born in Kent in 1833, Pearce originally worked at Chatham Dockyard before coming north to the then far greater opportunities offered on the Clyde for shipbuilding.

Under Pearce, Fairfield's became the biggest and probably the most technically advanced shipyard in the world, and his commercial success made him a millionaire several times over before his death at 55. In 1884, as sole partner in the firm, his income from the yard amounted to about £3,700 a week, a staggering sum when compared to the average wage for his 6,000 workers, which was about £1 a week. Pearce became Govan's first MP in 1885 (as a Conservative), and was created a baronet in 1887. His statue, known locally as 'The Black Man', stands opposite the PI on Govan Road, and was erected in 1894. After his death, the Pearce Institute was gifted to the people of Govan by his widow, with an endowment which amounted to about £1,000 a year to maintain it. This largesse did not, however, prevent the widow being still a merry one, as the bequest amounted to only about two per cent of the fortune left by Pearce. In his *History of Govan* (1905) TCF Brotchie wrote, as the Pearce Institute neared completion, *the institute is designed primarily for the use of the working men and women of Govan, and so many and varied are its sections –men's reading room and club, women's reading room and club, gymnasium, library, cooking and laundry departments– that the greatest benefits ought to accrue to the population. Its usefulness is doubled by the fact that it is entirely unsectarian.*

In addition to these facilities, the PI also had an Edwardian billiards room with Glasgow Style overhead lighting equipment, a cafeteria (no alcohol was served as the Institute was 'dry'), and a 600-seat theatre which later housed a magnificent organ. The Macleod Hall, as the theatre was called, was named after the Rev John Macleod, who was minister of Govan Old Church from 1875–1898. This Rev Macleod is not to be confused with the later incumbent of the same post from 1930 to 1938, George Macleod, a founder of the Christian-socialist Iona Community. Under the latter, the PI developed initiatives to combat the effects of the Depression in Govan in the 1930s, which put over half the population out of work and made a mockery of the town's motto, *Nihil sine Labore* – Nothing without Labour.

The Pearce Institute is an expression of the philanthropy practiced in pre-Welfare State days by Victorian and Edwardian capitalists. Such benevolence has also left us the Mitchell Library and the McLellan Galleries, among other bequests from Glasgow businessmen to their native city. Govan was littered with charitable endowments, from the Hills' Trust, dating from 1757, which eventually funded a school of the same name, to the Elder Library and Park, named after the previous owners of the Fairfield shipyard to Pearce himself). As well as ensuring immortality for the philanthropists, such institutions also allowed them to exert social control, e.g. over which games could be played in the park or which books could be read in the libraries. In the case of the Pearce Institute this meant no alcohol and strict gender segregation (the male and female sections of the building were initially physically separate and entered by separate doors), and in its early days the building certainly would not have been available for trade union meetings, amongst other things.

The PI was non-sectarian, but most of the Trustees were Church of Scotland, as well as others appointed from the Fairfield yard itself

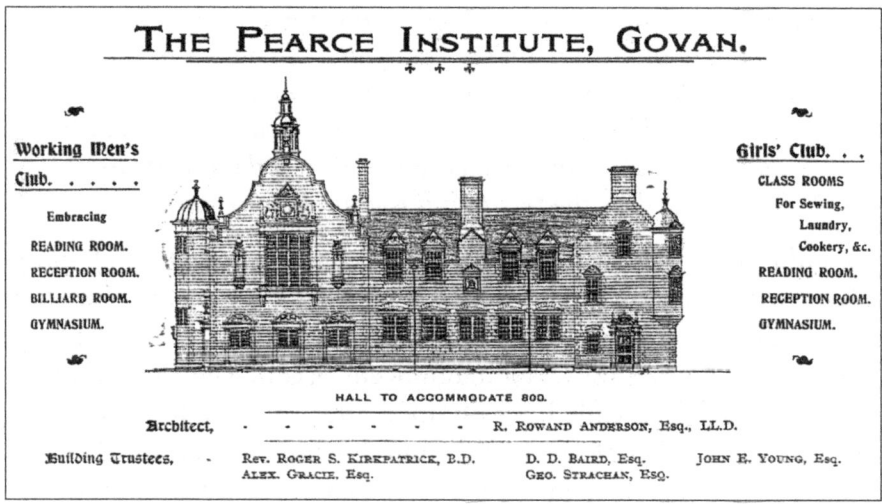

Pearce Institute, Govan
Programme cover from the laying of the memorial stone of the building in 1902 with the design of the completed building.

and from Glasgow University, with the management remaining in the hands of the minister and kirk session of Govan Old Kirk. In the *Greater Govan Press* *(December 2005) an assistant minister in the 1960s, Rev John Harvey, felt obliged to re-emphasise that 'contrary to some people's beliefs, it (the PI) was never run as a purely Protestant place'. These ties with the Church were cut in the 1980s when the PI became a charitable trust, and an attempt at restoring the building then raised about a million pounds for essential repairs which Lady Pearce's bequest could no longer cover.

The economic collapse of Govan in the 1980s and 1990s led to the closure of the Pearce in 2000, following that most of the Govan shipyards. As in the 1930s, today less than half of the working-age population of Govan is in employment, even though an exodus of people has reduced that population to less than half its level a century ago. Some, ignorant rather than malevolent, might suggest that the best thing to do with Govan would be to flatten it and build again; indeed, over the last 30 years 70 per cent of Govan's tenements have been demolished. The general image of Govan is a negative one, hardly helped by the Rab C Nesbit 'Wine Alley' caricatures which have graced our television screens since the late 1980s.

A century ago Govan had three theatres; that in the PI, another in the Govan Town Hall, built in 1901 to hold 2,000 people, and the Lyceum Theatre, which opened in 1899 with a performance of *Carmen* before 3,000 Govanites. The Govan Gaelic Choir, one of the best amateur choirs in Scotland, still exists, as does the Govan Fair, established by the Govan Weavers back in 1756. In addition, Govan used to boast Burns Clubs, political associations and the Reform Club, one of the oldest debating societies in Scotland. The *Govan Press*, which collapsed in 1983 as Govan imploded, published books, including Brotchie's *History of Govan*, as well as a local newspaper. All a far cry from 'wine alley'.

None of this even takes into account the role of Govan as one of the cradles of the Scottish labour movement. The early formation of trade unions in the shipyards was followed by its location as the centre of the Co-operative movement, when 5,000 people worked for the Scottish Co-operative Wholesale Society at Shieldhall in Govan. The area was one of the centres of the 1915 rent strike, and the only Glasgow constituency, except Gorbals, to elect a Labour MP, the ILP's Neil Maclean, in the Khaki Election of 1918. Militant working class politics continued until the UCS struggle of the early 1970s, in which the Govan shipyards again played a leading role.

This wealth of cultural activity was built on the enormous prosperity of the shipyards in Govan. But 'Govan's Glories' are not just in its industrial past, unrivalled though that is. Next to the PI, and also built by Robert Rowand Anderson, is Govan Old Parish Church, one of many which have stood on what has been a religious site for almost 1,500 years, since the monastery founded by St Constantine around 565 AD. There is an argument for Govan as a more important ecclesiastical site than Glasgow Cathedral, based largely upon Govan Old's unrivalled collection of early Christian and pre-Christian incised stones, including the Govan Sarcophagus. Govan Old Kirk is also A-Listed, and, since 2003, a scheduled monument. Current archeological thinking places early medieval Govan alongside Iona, St Andrews and Whithorn in terms of religious and political importance.

The PI reopened in 2003, and a programme of restoration work was undertaken. Grants from various organisations, including £335,000 from Communities Scotland, led to essential work being carried out on the roof and windows and to the restoration to working order of the clock on the front of the PI. With a further grant from Glasgow City Council for repair of the boilers and £105,000 from NHS Glasgow towards the regeneration of a community café, the restoration of this historic building has progressed well. This has led, in turn, to the use of the building by various community groups and commercial tenants, and the PI is increasingly becoming a location for arts-based activities. The reaction of local Govanites to the re-opening of the Pearce has been overwhelming. In the issue of *Greater Govan Press* cited above, there appears a collection of memories of the PI by older local residents, summed up in the words of one: 'I can never remember a time when the PI was not part of my life'. The Pearce Institute is a thread which runs through the fabric of Govan's rich history over the last 100 years, a fact evinced by the comment from a local that 'if they close the PI, they might just as well close Govan as well'.

Over the years, many of the functions of the Pearce have remained, others being added as Govan changed, and today the PI houses many of its traditional activities alongside economic training for young people, language centres for immigrant groups, and anti-poverty programmes. To mark its centenary in 2006, events were organised in the PI, and it was felt that the publication of a book of essays on the history of the building, and a collection of the reminiscences of those who have used its facilities, would be an appropriate commemoration. The outcome was *The Pearce Institute Centenary Book*, which will gladden the heart of Govanites at home or abroad, and which provides revealing insights into the community. It contains a wide variety of articles, including one by John Foster on William Pearce entitled 'Copper Trousered Philanthropist', but the book is not primarily about luminaries. It is about the ordinary, fine folk of Govan who created a vibrant community in the most difficult of circumstances, and who refused to let Govan die, or indeed to allow its still beating heart, the PI, to fail. Reading their patchwork of memories is a humbling but uplifting experience. As Govan experiences regeneration and redevelopment today, the PI will continue to make a major contribution to the process. I have had the fascinating experience, for the last six years or so, of basing a class on industrial history for students from Olso University in the PI, which, while it may be a modest contribution to the Institute's survival, provides a truly enlightening experience for the students involved.

The work on the Pearce is one of the building blocks in a wider attempt to restore central Govan under the Central Govan Action Plan. It is not widely known that central Govan has the greatest concentration of listed buildings and public sculptures in Glasgow outside the City Centre and West End, and too many sit now in a poor state of repair. These include the A-listed Govan Old Parish Church, the British Linen Bank at Govan Cross (designed by James Salmon Jr in 1900) and the Aitken Memorial Fountain now restored to its former glory as part of the upgrading of the civic space at Govan Cross. This has made a marked improvement to the look and feel of Govan Cross, for about £2.5 million – less than a banker's bonus.

A little further afield within Greater Govan lies the similarly A-graded Govan Graving Docks and Alexander 'Greek' Thomson's Walmer Crescent. Even Ibrox stadium, with its wonderful South Stand by Archibald Leitch, is B-listed. Indeed the central Govan area, with its largely intact tenement streets and historic Water Row, is now designated as a Conservation Area. This categorisation establishes a benchmark for the quality of conversion of old buildings to new use, and also for the quality of the new build that is planned for Govan, where there are schemes for a massive expansion of its housing sector, and hopes for growth of the area's population.

While I welcome the commitment and cash that is being devoted to Govan, it will all be of little benefit to local people unless efforts are made to ensure that a share of the new jobs are occupied by Govanites, and that social housing is expanded alongside private developments (elsewhere in Glasgow a failure to do this has resulted in the creation of middle-class enclaves alongside working-class ghettoes). The Central Govan Action Plan has expressed its commitment to expanding the housing association rented sector alongside other developments. Conservation needs to be allied to social regeneration and inclusion, and the Peace Institute is striving towards this goal, fulfilling the words above its entrance:

> THIS IS A HOUSE OF FRIENDSHIP. THIS IS A HOUSE OF SERVICE.
> FOR FAMILIES. FOR LONELY FOLK. FOR THE PEOPLE OF GOVAN.
> FOR THE STRANGERS OF THE WORLD. WELCOME.

The Pearce Institute has an important role to play in a Govan which values its past and now has the opportunity, after decades of despair, to develop hope for its future.

For further information on the Pearce Institute contact: 0141 445 6007, mail@pearceinstitute.org.uk · www.pearceinstitute.org.uk

For Govan Old Church see: www.govanold.org.uk
govanold.pc@virgin.net · 0141 440 2466

There is a fine pamphlet, *The Govan Heritage Trail,* illustrating a guided walk round some of Govan's most notable buildings and monuments, which is available from the Elder Park Library in Govan (0141 445 1047). There is also a further pamphlet on Elder Park and its sculptures called *Elder Park Heritage Trail.*

* The *Greater Govan Press* referred to here is a recently-appeared freesheet, not the newspaper which shut down in 1983 after a century of existence.

CHAPTER ELEVEN

Alex Ferguson's Govan

ALEX FERGUSON IS one of the most successful club managers in British, and possibly even European, football history. His achievements with Manchester United are unparalleled, but – at least from my perspective as an Aberdeen FC supporter – possibly more impressive was his raising of that provincial Scottish club to a position of dominance in the Scottish game for much of the 1980s and to the pinnacle of European football with the winning of the Cup-Winners' Cup against the mighty Real Madrid in 1983. While others may debate what made Fergie such a footballing genius, in his mind, as becomes clear to readers of his autobiography, *Managing My Life* (2000), there is no mystery at all. It is all down to Govan, and his upbringing in what was formerly the shipbuilding capital of the world:

> I have no doubt it is true, and I am sure too, that any success I have had in handling men, and in creating a culture of loyalty and commitment in teams I have managed owes much to my upbringing among the working men of Clydeside.

Doubtless Bill Shankly and Jock Stein, who came from Scottish mining communities, would also have attributed their success in part to their backgrounds.

This chapter – 'Alex Ferguson's Govan' – is so-called advisedly. Glasgow figures very marginally in his autobiography, to the extent that geographically unaware readers of the book might struggle to realise that Govan is actually a part of Glasgow. In this Ferguson is a typical Govanite, for it is probably the area of Glasgow with the strongest local identity, and almost exactly 100 years after Govan was annexed by the city this identity still survives, as was explored in the previous two chapters. The local mindset is captured by Fergie when he states that 'to call Govan a district is an insult'. However, this local patriotism does not here breed parochialism, as can too often be the case, for Govan was the cradle of the labour, co-operative and trade union movements in Scotland, and intense local pride combined with wider perspectives informs Fergie himself. He is possibly the area's most famous son, although the early-1970s leader of the UCS Work-In Jimmy Reid, at whose funeral Ferguson officiated, must come a close second.

It has been a number of years since Alex Ferguson moved away from Govan, though in some ways mentally he has never left it, and he still revisits the area frequently. When Manchester United played at Ibrox not too long ago, he took the players on a tour of Govan in the team bus. In those decades since Ferguson left, Govan has seen a heart-aching decline in its industrial base, with the closure of most of the shipyards and engineering works. Its population, sitting now at a much-depleted 30,000, is much less than half of what it was when Fergie was a lad kicking about the streets. Perhaps even more saddening is that much of the Govan Ferguson knew has been obliterated from memory by the demolition of many of the old tenement buildings (over three quarters of the area's tenements were demolished in the 1960s and 1970s), factories and other physical landmarks.

When he was born in 1941, Govan was a tightly-packed, high population density area of mainly tenement dwellings. The three great yards (Stephens', Fairfields and Harland and Wolff) fronting the River Clyde were working flat-out at wartime production after the depression of the 1930s had seen four in five Govan men out of work. For 20 years thereafter not a lot changed as the yards continued booming in the post-war reconstruction period, and Govan appeared to have recovered from the crisis of the 1930s. At this point in Govan's history, despite the expansion of council house building after 1945, most of the old tenements still stood, and that is the Govan Ferguson grew up in, one that remains now only in memory and photographs. There is *just* enough left of Fergie's Govan to merit a perambulation around scenes and sights that might one day become staging posts on a pilgrimage for Manchester United fans in the same way as they have been for a long time part of this Aberdeen fan's Govan walkabouts. After all, Liverpool fans visit the former mining town of Glenbuck in Ayrshire, now a ghost town, to pay homage to Bill Shankly.

Linthouse FC. Govan's Football Heritage 1.
From the earliest days teams were formed based on areas and workplaces in Govan. Here we have Linthouse with the trainer/manager dressed in a bowler hat, a sign of authority in the shipyards and on the pitch. Ferguson never needed such an outward mark of his authority.

No. 667 Govan Road no longer exists. Though he was born in an inter-war council house in Drumoyne, about a mile away on the southern fringe of Govan, Alex Ferguson spent most of his early years in his parents' rented tenement flat at this address. From the front windows the occupants looked out across Govan Road, beyond which was the Harland and Wolff shipyard. This was the first of the great Govan yards to close – in 1962 – its site later filled and overbuilt by a 1970s social housing development. The Govan Road tenements which backed onto the yard were also demolished and replaced by what passes as a 'landscaped' area comprising grass and a few trees. It is now dead land, serving little purpose. The Ferguson block stood across the thoroughfare, roughly where the Fire Station is today, where Neptune Street meets Govan Road.

Although his father was a skilled worker in Fairfield's, the Fergusons still had to sub-let part of their flat to an Irish couple to make ends meet. In one respect, however, they were lucky; unlike many Govan tenements, theirs had an indoor toilet. Their neighbours, the Laws, were not so fortunate, and kept 'about 16 people' in a room and kitchen. Almost all of the tenements on this stretch of Govan Road were demolished and only now, more than 30 years later, are some of the vacant sites being built upon.

If Fergie's house is gone, his primary school is still there – though only just. Proceed up Orkney Street from Govan Road and you come to Broomloan Road and Broomloan Primary School, or rather the abandoned and boarded up Edwardian sandstone building which formerly served as a school. Depopulation and a declining birth rate left Govan with a large surplus of buildings – including schools – of which this is one example. In more salubrious areas of Glasgow the building might become converted into modern apartments, but not here, where the costs of such a renovation are unlikely to be recouped by the resulting income in rent or property sales. Broomloan Road was a rough school in Fergie's day – he notes that it had a higher proportion of its graduates on probation than any other Glasgow primary. Nonetheless he appears to have been a fairly well-behaved kid and enjoyed his schooling, speaking very highly of his teachers, especially one Elizabeth Thomson, on whom he had a crush and with whom he kept up a long contact afterwards. The strong family ties of his respectable working-class background probably help to account for Alex's good behaviour when so many of his peers were to follow more errant paths. He appears to have been fairly skilled at neither offending overtly nor becoming too involved with the local petty criminals. One story he relates tells of how he skilfully evaded the unwelcome attentions of one Willie Bennet, nicknamed 'The Devil' and later destined to die in a Govan pub brawl. Ferguson met him again when, as Aberdeen manager, he chaired a quiz for the inmates at Peterhead Prison. Managing Eric

Cantona or Wayne Rooney must have been easy after experiences such as this.

If you continue to the end of Broomloan Road, you will light upon a more famous place about which Ferguson has less warm memories: Ibrox Park, home of Rangers Football Club. Religious sectarianism was anathema in the Ferguson household. His father was a lapsed Protestant and secular socialist who married a Catholic wife. The Ferguson brothers supported Rangers whilst the father (whom the young Alex greatly admired) was Celtic-minded. Ferguson himself also later married a Catholic. Fergie came initially to Rangers' serious attention when, as a St Johnstone player, he became the first person to score a hat trick against the Gers at Ibrox. It is part of the deeply ingrained belief of Scottish football fans that if you play a good game against Rangers, they buy you, and then stick you in their reserves. There is an element of truth to this in Fergie's case. Though he would later play for Rangers from 1967–1969, Fergie's time at Ibrox was fraught with difficulties and conflicts, and he parted from the club on less than amicable terms. Fergie himself feels that sectarian bias made his time less successful at Ibrox than it might have been. In the 1960s Rangers had a 'No Catholics' rule, and they operated a culture which saw someone who had married a Catholic as failing in his duties as a 'True Blue'. When Ferguson's form dipped, he was on a shakier peg than others might have been. Ferguson recalls that one of the Rangers directors asked him, when they first met after his signing for the club, what his wife's religion was. He also argues that the weak-willed manager at the time, Davie White, was under the influence of the sectarian PR man Willie Allison. Eventually, after 'a humiliating period when I was condemned to third-team football against the likes of Glasgow Transport and Glasgow University', he was transferred from the club. In the end the loss was more Rangers' than Ferguson's. The conflict and the bitterness it left with him probably contributed to his turning down the job of Rangers manager when it was offered to him after his outstanding success with Aberdeen in the 1980s.

For a working-class area, Govan has an exceptional collection of public sculptures. Although one of Ferguson has recently been erected at Old Trafford, he is unlikely ever to be captured in sculpture outside Ibrox Park. There does stand there, however, a fine statue of John Grieg, his head lowered in grief and mourning, commemorating the Ibrox Disaster of 1971. One wonders how Fergie feels about the current plight of Rangers FC, whose dubious financial practises brought the club to the brink of extinction in 2012, and who at the time of writing are currently playing in the Scottish Second Division.

Govan's Old Firm. Govan's Football Heritage 2.
Not all Govan teams were based on district or workplace allegiance, as can be seen from this image of Govan's own Old Firm in the 1950s, which mirrored the religious divisions in the district.

Travelling west along Edmiston Drive you soon come to Helen Street. Proceeding then southwards down Helen Street brings you to Harmony Row, a place which has fonder – and continuing – footballing associations with Alex Ferguson. After being 'fitba daft' at Govan High School, playing with the school team and also in the Life Boys and later Boys Brigade line-ups, Ferguson's footballing odyssey continued here at the Harmony Row Boys' Club. Fergie's talent secured him a place in the team which played in the Glasgow Boys' Club League. As well as learning football skills there, the team had to learn street survival tactics. Their greatest rivals were Bridgeton Boys' Club, and when Harmony Row won 4–1 at an away game, the rumour soon spread that the victorious visitors would be attacked after the game. On the final whistle the entire Harmony Row team ran for a tram, which luckily arrived just before an enraged mob caught up with them. On another occasion, Fergie scored four goals to help Harmony beat Bridgeton in the Boys' Cup Final by 7–0. This time trouble occurred when they arrived back home and were attacked by a razor gang emerging from a fairground in Govan, and a full-scale battle ensued. With experiences like this under his belt, it is little wonder that Alex has often appeared unfazed by what later footballing life threw at him. Despite the passing of much time, Fergie still has strong links with the Harmony Row club, which has recently acquired new state-of-the-art facilities a far cry from the ash and blaize 'puggy' pitch upon which Fergie played.

Further down Harmony Row you arrive in central Govan and, a little to the right, at Govan Cross – for generations the heart of the community. With Govan's economic decline and depopulation, this formerly bustling area became something akin to a wasteland, housing for many years a bleak 1970s shopping centre and a derelict area surrounding the former pride of Govan – the Aitken Memorial Fountain. A wholly different picture could be found some 50 years ago, when the area was, according to Ferguson,

> alive with noise and movement as organ grinders, fruit sellers, backcourt singers and bookies' runners competed for whatever few shilling people had to spare... Maybe I was easily enthralled, but at times I felt I was in the midst of a carnival.

In the last couple of years, the long-derelict areas around here have been gradually filling up with new housing. This is mainly social housing, given the economic crisis facing private house building, but still the re-population of Govan is finally beginning. Hopefully Govan Cross will become again what it was in Fergie's day – the centre of a thriving community.

Westwards along Govan Road from the Cross sits the Pearce Institute, another building which has Ferguson associations past and present. When Alex was a boy, this was the community heart of Govan, with clubs and associations meeting there. He learned to play five-a-side football there in a sunken gymnasium hall (it was meant to have been a swimming pool, but there was no money to carry the necessary aquatic works out). When the PI was faced with closure ten years ago, Ferguson backed the campaign to keep the building open, and today he retains strong links with the PI, and provided the *Foreword* to its Centenary Celebration publication (a publication to which I was also honoured to contribute). A painting of Ferguson hangs inside the PI in recognition of his efforts.

Further westwards again from the PI, after passing through the remaining area of Govan tenements, lies Fairfields shipyard, where Fergie's father and brother worked. This enterprise remains open today, the last working yard in Govan, but with a labour force of about 1,500, compared to the 5,000 there when it provided the Ferguson family's income. Fergie talks of waiting for his father after a shift, when thousands of men came out in a tide of 'bunnets' (cloth caps), trying to recognise his dad by his peculiar walk. The loss of this industry, the fabric of Govan's existence, is felt as a personal pain. On the very first page of his autobiography Alex comments that when, in the 1970s,

> Jimmy Reid and James Airlie and other outstanding trade unionists lost their brave fight to save the industry from the virtual extinction that has overtaken it, an irreplaceable element was removed from Govan life forever.

Ferguson's house in Cheshire is tellingly called 'Fairfields' after the yard, and he has commented 'I like plenty of echoes of Govan around me'. The former palatial offices of the yard, described as the most opulent shipyard offices in the UK, lay unused and empty for many years, but have now been designated for use as workspaces. The restoration of possibly Govan's most iconic building, the nerve-centre of its most famous shipyard, is at time of writing under way.

Across the road from Fairfields is the Elder Park. This was Govan's small green lung and during the summer Glasgow Fair holidays it was thronged with those who could not afford a trip away from the area. Even in the 1960s there were many kids in Govan for whom the holidays meant a summer in Elder Park rather than a week or the odd day 'Doon the Watter' on the Clyde Coast. Elder Park is a flat green place, not one of Glasgow's finest visuals, but it has an interesting collection of public sculptures, most relating to the area's shipbuilding history, and a Heritage Trail around these was recently created. A walk through the park takes you to Langlands Road, where Govan High formerly stood, the local senior secondary at that time and Fergie's secondary school. Govan High is another local institution which Alex Ferguson maintains links with, having been the guest of honour at its centenary celebrations in 2010, where he recalled the strong influence on him of the school team's coach, George Symington.

Fergie was not to follow his father and brother into the yards. Although illness had interrupted his education and probably prevented him getting the necessary qualifications to go on to university, he achieved enough grades to enable him to move a step up from the yards and engage as a skilled toolmaker in factories on the Hillingdon estate, a couple of miles west of Govan. This was better paid, cleaner and less physically demanding work than that found in the shipyards. He completed his apprenticeship in toolmaking and was an active trade unionist before becoming a full-time footballer. He took part in several industrial disputes, including as the apprentices' shop steward at Remington-Rand in 1961 during a national strike, later becoming tool room shop steward and bringing the men out in an (unsuccessful) strike to demand re-instatement of a worker sacked for political reasons. Though he did not share the man's communist beliefs, Ferguson stood by union principles and led a strike against the dismissal. He comments, 'I was proud of the workers who made a stand along with me and that period of my life gives me lasting satisfaction'. If Ferguson had not become such a successful football manager it is not difficult to imagine that his political convictions and management skills might have enabled him to become a powerful and prominent trade union official.

Alex Ferguson has achieved more than most in his life and many people – especially in Govan – would feel that he has everything he could possibly want. Much of what he has gained he puts down to his Govan roots, even while recognising that the Govan which nurtured him has gone. There is one thing he cannot have, and that is to go back in time, for the places he came from exist only in memory. Ferguson describes fondly the people he grew up amongst:

> Ambition had nothing to do with their lives. Survival was the essence, yet there was incredible warmth of fellow feeling among them, a loyalty that was as deep as the marrow. I wish I could revisit, however briefly, the sense of community that existed in the Govan of my childhood. It could be a rough world but there were wonderful values at the heart of it. Loyalty has been the anchor of my life and it is something that I learned in Govan.

It is to be hoped that the new Govan which is slowly rising from the ashes of the old will be able to build on these values of loyalty and community, which despite the ravages of the last 40 years are far from extinct, and have a representative in Alex Ferguson.

CHAPTER TWELVE

Mental Memorials: The Socialist City Centre

I HAD THE opportunity to visit East Berlin on various occasions in the 1980s, at that time when it was officially designated as Berlin, Capital of the German Democratic Republic. The authorities made much of their stated aim of creating a 'socialist city centre' in the part of the city they controlled, which included almost all of the former central areas of unified Berlin. Now, leaving aside what was meant by this in planning terms – streets, public spaces, buildings and so forth – the use of the phrase 'socialist city centre' clearly implied what was intended in terms of iconography. It primarily meant the removal of memorials, statues and street names which were politically suspect, and their replacement with mementos to figures of labour and socialist history (as well as to 'progressive' bourgeois individuals). It is surprising on subsequent returns to Berlin post-reunification to see how much of this iconography remains. Memorials to Marx, Liebknecht and Thaelemann still people its city streets.

Comparisons are invidious, but in relation to Glasgow's socialist and labour history, there is almost nothing to match commemoration of the past as seen in Berlin, despite the fact that for the great bulk of the last 80 years Glasgow has been run by the Labour Party. The 'socialist city centre' of Glasgow is peopled by unseen memorials and these exist only – or almost only – as a mental map in the minds of the knowledgeable. Armed with such a knowledge, a linear walk of a couple of miles can be made which begins at one 'station of the cross', Charing Cross station, ends at another, Bridgeton Cross, and takes us to largely uncommemorated places which were significant in the political history of proletarian Glasgow.

Memorials, icons and commemorations abound on the Mitchell Library, at its current Granville Street entrance. This frontage was

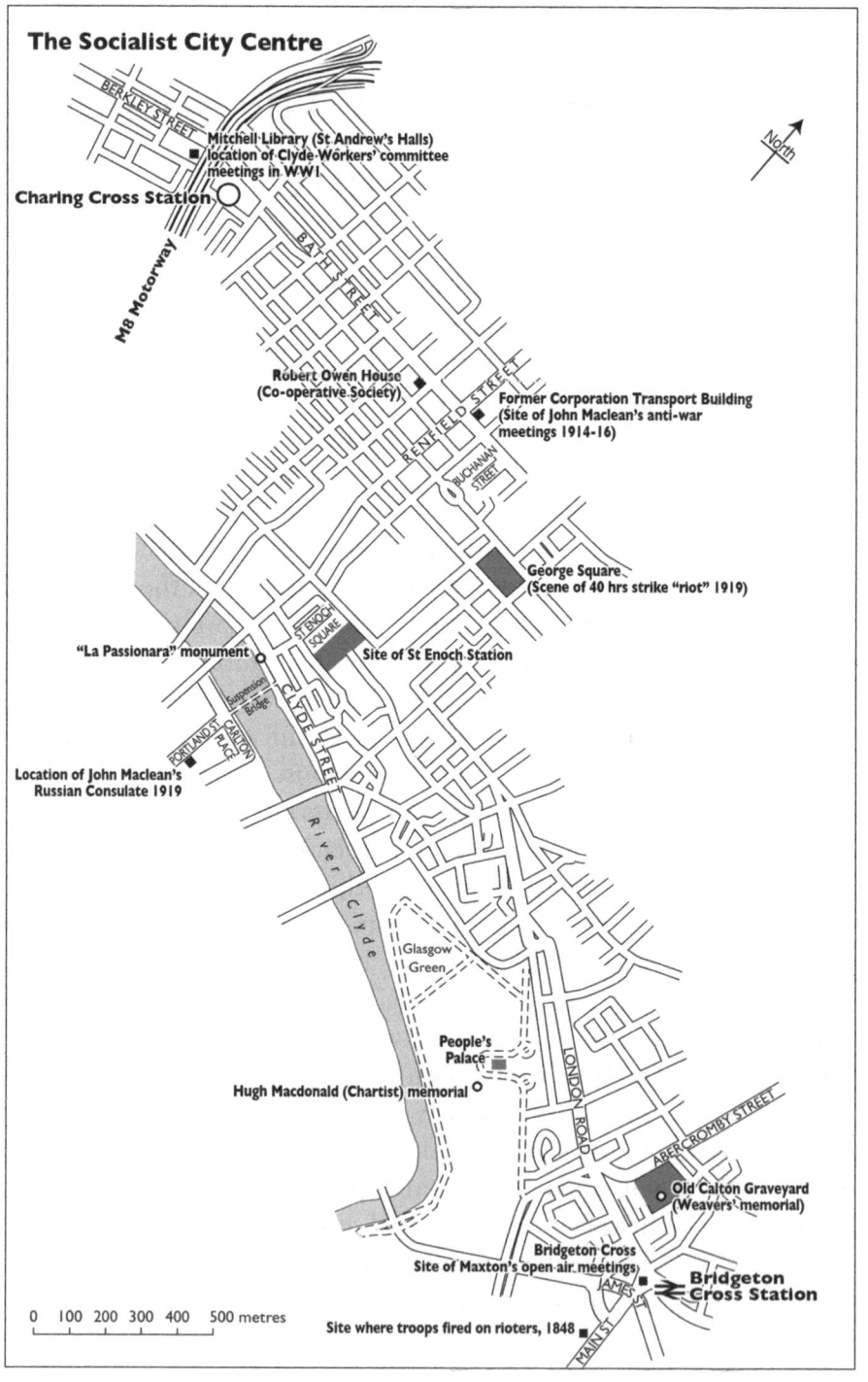

originally the entrance to the St Andrew's Halls, destroyed internally by fire in 1962. The exterior remains and is well worth a studious deconstruction. Statues of Homer, Dante and Shakespeare represent *Literature,* and of Michelangelo, Leonardo and Raphael *Art,* while frame panels honour the names of Newton, Watt, Bach, Mozart and Beethoven. However there is no commemoration of the fact that within these walls almost a century ago, when they still contained the St Andrew's Halls, took place an event of potential world-historical importance. In 1914 the conflict between British and German Imperialism had led to the outbreak of a Great War, which the socialist parties of Europe had previously pledged themselves to oppose by a general strike. Almost without exception, the socialist parties and the trade unions capitulated to national chauvinism and endorsed the war. But that did not end the problems of the warmongers; they still had to win it.

Boosting industrial output to prosecute the war meant changing labour practices, largely destroying the gains built up by the skilled working class over decades, and replacing skilled with unskilled labour in the munitions factories (dilution). On Clydeside an uneasy alliance of craft-conscious skilled workers opposed to dilution and their socialist shop stewards (mainly members of the Socialist Labour Party) opposed to the war emerged in the shape of the Clyde Workers Committee (CWC). In December 1915 Lloyd George, Minister of Munitions, came to Glasgow to speak at a meeting of munitions workers and their CWC representatives in the St Andrew's Halls. He received a hostile reception. The 'highest paid munitions worker in the country' was shouted down, denied a hearing, and exited the building to a rendition of *The Red Flag*. It looked like dilution might not be agreed, with incalculable consequences, including possible German victory. The alternative was martial law, widely proposed at the time, with the potential for large-scale civil unrest. The fate of the British Empire hung in the balance with the dilution crisis; this was a point when history could have turned. However, betrayal by some of the CWC leaders, in particular by David (later Lord) Kirkwood at Parkhead Forge, meant that opposition to dilution collapsed and the introduction of the strategy resulted in a huge productivity increase. It is unlikely that the ruling Labour Party in Glasgow, which, like its national parent party, has supported every war launched by the British state since 1914, would commemorate here a moment when an alternative to war seemed possible.

About ten minutes down Bath Street towards the town centre one comes across an unimpressive modern building called Robert Owen House, the present headquarters of the Co-operative Society, named after one of the founders of the ideas of social and industrial co-operation. When one compares this with their former head office and warehouses in Kingston, built on a palatial style a century ago, one can see that the Co-op has struggled and declined in the intervening period. The Socialist Labour Party were accused of being violent revolutionaries when in fact they were syndicalists, believing that social change would come through 'workers' control' of industry. On the other hand, one could never have accused the Co-op, with its vision of the gradual spread of peaceful co-operative production and distribution, of being revolutionaries. But even the Co-op was so radicalised by the Great War that on May Day in 1918 they gave their 5,000 workers at Shieldhall a paid day off to join the strike against the war, an event we will revisit later in this chapter.

Just a little further on, across the road at the junction of Bath Street and Renfield Street, stands a building which used to house the Glasgow Corporation Tramways Department. For much of the Great War, when he was not in prison or on a political tour, John Maclean held Sunday evening meetings here to denounce the war as an imperialist conflict in which the workers of the world had no interest. In any other location he might have been shouted down or even attacked (as Keir Hardie was, by the South Wales miners who had previously elected him as their MP, when he opposed the war). As it was, because of solid support for Maclean's views, Glasgow was for a while the only place in the British Empire where someone could stand up and denounce the war without immediate consequences. Proceeding warily, the authorities initially arrested Maclean and offered the choice of a £5 fine or five days in prison, which latter option he accepted. In February 1916 he was again arrested after a Bath Street meeting, tried, and sentenced under the Defence of the Realm Act to three years' penal servitude. There is no statue of Maclean here or anywhere in Glasgow (though there is a memorial stone near his Pollokshaws birthplace, and a plaque on the City Halls in Candleriggs commemorates his work with the unemployed agitation in 1921).

If we now head down Buchanan Street, and take a left turn into George Street and George Square, we will find statues of various eminent – and many pretty un-eminent – bourgeois politicians, capitalists and generals, not forgetting of course Victoria and Albert, and, commonplace throughout Glasgow, James Watt. The only memorial of interest to anyone of a radical bent would be that to Rabbie Burns. The square also hosts the Cenotaph commemorating the city's dead of the British 20th-century wars, a number sadly way above Glasgow's corresponding proportion of the British population. Recently the Council came up with the idea of sweeping all these icons away in order to create an Events Space to host spectacles which would, in turn, help bolster the city's diminished coffers. Understandably, opposition to this idea came from various quarters and it has been dropped, and replaced by a simple clean-up of the square. Personally I would keep Watt, Burns and Walter Scott and get rid of the rest, replacing them with ones of people from all walks of life who have really contributed to the city's heritage – not just its working class heritage, but its scientific legacy as well.

George Square features more prominently in the memory of Glasgow socialists than anywhere else because of a single event: the George Square Riot of 1919. At a time when the Spartacist Rising in Berlin had just been put down and its leaders, Liebknecht and Luxemburg, murdered, the authorities in the City Chambers and in Whitehall were seriously enough concerned by the threat of a 'Bolshevik Rising' in Glasgow that local troops were confined to barracks and others from England brought into the city. Tanks were stationed in the Saltmarket and armed soldiers were on guard in the City Chambers. What faced them was the threat posed by a general strike (which failed to extend much beyond Clydeside) in favour of the introduction of the 40-hour week to allow the assimilation of demobbed soldiers back into employment. Behind the strike the authorities saw the hydra of revolution, and whilst its leaders were in the Chambers debating with the city authorities on 31 January, the strikers were attacked by baton-wielding police and serious rioting ensued.

The leaders of the strike, many of whom were subsequently beaten by police and arrested, had had no such insurrectionary intent, and the localised action petered out when troops and tanks arrived in the city afterwards. Though some of the strike leaders, notably Willie Gallacher, were later to say that a revolutionary moment had been missed, I feel that John Maclean made one of his last sound judgements when he stated that the movement had been defeated 'more by the lack of working-class ripeness than batons, tanks and machine guns'. The future in Glasgow lay not with the extreme left, but with Labourism. In 1933 Pat Dollan became Glasgow's first Labour Provost and the party has scarcely been out of office in these Chambers since.

Heading down Queen Street you come to Argyll Street and the massive complex of the St Enoch shopping centre. Older Glaswegians will recall when the St Enoch Square here, with its still in place Jacobean Underground Station, also contained the much larger St Enoch Station, the main departure point for the journey south in bygone days. It was from here that the Red Clydesiders departed for Westminster in 1922 after their astonishing election victory when they, in the form of the Independent Labour Party, took eight of Glasgow's then 12 parliamentary seats. At that time the Labour Party was a federation of different groups, with the ILP very much on the left wing. After the adoption of Clause IV in 1918 committing Labour to social ownership, the Red Clydesiders had great hopes for the party. These hopes were shattered by events from 1924–1931, and it was at the end of this period that the ILP left the Labour Party. The ILP was very different from the groups which had been active during the War, and they had played very little role in the industrial agitation which had taken place then, despite being prominent in the Rent Strike of 1915. Nevertheless, they won the overwhelming support of Glasgow working-class voters in the 1920s and to some extent blocked the advance of the Communist Party which was emerging more prominently in places like Motherwell, Clydebank and Greenock. A huge crowd gathered to cheer the Clydesiders off to London. Once there they, especially James Maxton, enlivened the proceedings of parliament with fiery rhetoric, but in reality the ILP was no more revolutionary than the Co-operative Society.

The failure of the Communist Party to make even a modest political breakthrough in Glasgow, either at the parliamentary or the local council level, is interesting given its success elsewhere on Clydeside, but the party did become powerful in the trade union movement, especially at shop steward level, and in wider political campaigning. Their influence was clear during the Spanish Civil War, when a very large number of Scots went to fight Franco in Spain, a disproportionate number of those being from Glasgow. Despite its Popular Front rhetoric, the International Brigade was heavily dominated politically and numerically by the Communist Party. It is therefore appropriate that the monument to the International Brigadiers on Clyde Street, reached quickly by heading down

Maxton Election poster
A smiling Maxton with Bunnet and Bairn. From the 1920s when he became Brigton's firebrand MP.

Dixon Street from St Enoch Square, commemorates Dolores Ibarutti ('La Passionara') one of the leaders of the Spanish Communist Party during and after the Civil War. Arthur Dooley, himself a communist and a former welder, executed the statue in 1979. Just across the chain bridge here is Portland Street where briefly in 1919 John MacLean was a consul for the new Soviet Government.

A walk along Clyde Street brings the iconographer of the unseen to Glasgow Green, which, like George Square, has no lack of monuments spread around its territory. There is one to Horatio Nelson, one to William Collins (the tee-total campaigner, biblical publisher and former Glasgow Provost), the world-significant Doulton terracotta fountain of 1888, celebrating the British Empire and – of course – a statue of James Watt, of whom there are more in Glasgow than of any other individual. But despite the fact that the Green has been the scene of working-class demonstrations for almost two centuries – from those of the Chartists, and earlier, for the right to vote, through mobilisations against the Great War and the Free Speech campaigns of the 1930s, to rallies around the UCS work-in in the early 1970s – there is precious little proletarian iconography on the Green itself. For that you have to go inside the People's Palace, which stands there. Amongst the most important demonstrations to take place on this site was the May Day march in 1917, when 80,000 people took to the streets to demand an end to the war, and express solidarity with the Russian Revolution. Even more significant was the demonstration of the following year when, for the first and last time, May Day took the form of a strike on a working day, whose main themes for the 100,000 who downed tools were again working class international solidarity and an end to the imperialist holocaust. After the rally a large section of the crowd marched to the nearby Duke Street prison to demand the release of Maclean, who had been arrested again. The walls of that prison, still standing, do not carry a memorial to his heroic fight against the war, which I feel is an omission made in error.

There is one memorial of relevance to us on the Green. The Hugh MacDonald Memorial, behind the People's Palace, commemorates a man who was a prominent Chartist in Glasgow in the 1840s as well as a radical journalist, poet, and early urban-edge rambler. Chartism, a movement seeking to gain the vote for the male working class, was widespread in Glasgow, and generally moderate. Some of the workers who supported the Chartists were, however, prone to take direct action in times of distress. At a mass meeting of the unemployed on 6 March 1848 on the Green, calling for aid for those in distress, two speakers, Smith and Crossin, denounced the government and the city authorities and called upon the hungry to take what they needed. Mass rioting over the east end and city centre occurred, shops were looted, as was a gunsmiths at Glasgow Cross, where the rioters started to erect a barricade before being interrupted when the troops arrived. The protestors retreated towards Bridgeton. There, at the junction of Main Street and John (now Tullis) Street, the troops fired on the demonstrators, killing at least one man and wounding many others. Smith and Crossin were sentenced to 18 years transportation each, and a large number of other rioters faced lesser terms. Meanwhile Captain Smart, the man who had ordered the troops to fire without first using blanks or firing shots over the demonstrators' heads as he was legally obliged to do, was made Chief Constable of Glasgow.

There is no memorial to the victims of the 1848 incident, but just off the Green, at the bottom of Abercromby Street in the Calton Old Graveyard, there is a memorial to the Calton weavers killed in the strike of 1787, erected by their fellow weavers some time afterwards. They had stopped work when the cloth masters reduced their piece rates and the struggle is generally regarded as the first stirrings of the labour movement in Scotland. Sadly, the memorial is now largely illegible, and a replacement created at a later date is also damaged. The graveyard was lucky to be included in the Bridgeton town centre regeneration scheme of the Scottish Government, and has been tidied up. The surrounding pavements in Caithness flagstone feature slabs inlaid with historical information. I feel that it would be fitting, as well as commemorating the martyred Calton Weavers, if there could be some kind of memorial erected here to the victims of 1848.

The regeneration of Bridgeton Cross, to provide a focal point for a community which certainly has its stresses and problems, has been a major success. The Umbrella (a cast iron extravaganza) has been fully restored, and its clock now works. The former Olympia Cinema (and before that Music Hall), which had lain derelict for two decades, has been restored to community multi-use and the whole area landscaped with metal seating and flagged. A new icon has been raised, emblazoned with the word LUV, and on closer inspection it turns out to be a memorial to Robert Burns, who was a great hero of the original weavers in these parts, and who in later heavy industrial times maintained his local popularity. Then Bridgeton had the biggest Burns Club in the world. I was slightly saddened to see that John Maxton, MP for Bridgeton from 1922 until his death in 1945, is not here remembered in any way, despite the fact that he held open air political meetings at Bridgeton Cross for much of his life. He was well-loved in the area and was, despite his faults, a man of political integrity who deserves to be remembered. I have given talks in Bridgeton and shown images of Maxton, and was pleased that many people – the majority not yet born when Maxton died – recognised who he was from the pictures I showed them even before I had mentioned his name. But that knowledge will fade, and would appear to be fading already, given his absence from any mention in the regeneration of the area around the Umbrella. A campaign for a Maxton statue at the Cross would have my support.

In raising awareness of the seen and unseen memorials of past struggles we aim to keep alive the memory of those who fought for social justice, a memory that can help inspire present and future generations to do likewise.

A more detailed and elaborated walk between Brigton Cross and the Mitchell Library can be found by clicking on 'Walks' at the Glasgow Friends of Mayday website – http://may1st.org.uk

CHAPTER THIRTEEN

A Night at the Opry: an Evening Doon the Watter

NOTWITHSTANDING EDINBURGH'S political status, Glasgow is the undoubted musical capital of Scotland. It is the home of Scottish Opera, of the Scottish National Orchestra, of the BBC Scottish Symphony Orchestra, of Scottish Ballet (there's music there too), and of the Royal Conservatoire of Scotland. But it is not only in the realm of High Culture that its musical credentials are impeccable. In Celtic Connections, held annually to brighten the gloom of January and February nights, the city has one of the globally pre-eminent festivals of World Music. Glasgow boasts a tradition in rock and pop music which stretches back to Alex Harvey and Gerry Rafferty – now both much more appreciated than in their lifetime – and continues right up to Simple Minds, The Fratellis, Hue and Cry, Deacon Blue, Wet Wet Wet, Texas and Franz Ferdinand. It is thus no exaggeration to say that Glasgow (and its contiguous environs) occupies a similar position in popular music to that enjoyed by Liverpool in the 1960s.

However, your writer is a man whose musical tastes have been focussed for the last 40 years on keeping up with Bob Dylan's latest releases, coupled with an untutored musical ear listening a few times a year on LP – and now CD – to a complete performance of Wagner's *Ring* cycle. Though I had fully intended to devote a chapter to a ramble around the physical locations of Glasgow's music scene, today and in the past, it was very soon apparent to me that I lack the qualifications to do so. The urban *flaneur* is someone who, away from libraries and books, encounters and comprehends the city through its physical and social manifestations. He 'reads the signatures of all things', as Stephen Daedalus, of James Joyce's *Ulysses*, says of himself when wandering around Dublin. I quickly became aware that I did not have the knowledge to be able to stroll around all the musical haunts of the city and make any more than casual comments on the exteriors of its buildings – from the Theatre Royal to the now multiplexed site of the Apollo, from Barrowland to the Royal Concert Hall – being sadly unequipped to say anything about the musical significance of what has taken place inside them. To read the signatures of all things you have to be literate, and I was, and am, musically illiterate. Hopefully someone more capable will attempt the fascinating and essential task of initiating an overview of Glasgow as the Music City, but it is a not a project to be undertaken by someone who heard Paulo Nutini in Barga, Italy when he was still an unknown and thought, 'this fella should stick to the day job', only to find the lad mega famous a year later. Nevertheless, even for the musically challenged such as myself, there are opportunities for immersing oneself in aspects of the city's musical scene.

In the interval you do not go for canapés or a glass of chilled white wine. You head for the Chuck Wagon where you can properly tuck in to beans on toast, swilled down with some beer largely made from chemicals, for here you are not amongst those in smart suits or evening dresses, but mingling with Clydeside Cowboys and Cowgals outfitted in checked shirts and jeans, the more devoted aficionados sporting six-guns and cowboy boots. This is not Scottish Opera in Glasgow city centre, but the Grand Old Opry at the Paisley Road Toll. It is not for the faint-hearted. After the first half warm-up band comes the interval, and then the Shoot-Out, in which the Outlaws from Oatlands and Baddies from Bellshill compete to be fastest on the draw. But we are not really in America, so it's blanks they fire. Two Gun Slim opines to me that 'ye hiv tae keep yer holster lubricated', and shows me his weapons before going off to be gunned down by the Kansas Kid. The second half features some local or not so local Country and Western band trying to turn the south side into the Wild West. The general dancing is interspersed by line dancing (locally known as The Slosh), which women perform around a line of handbags abandoned on the sticky floor. Things get frantic towards the end and I decline Texas Rose's invitation to dance, though agreeing with her that 'a guid night, that's whit ye get here, a guid night'. The evening's entertainments are rounded off by the lowering of the Confederate Flag (I console myself that the iconography of this is totally lost on the local punters – they are hardly Ku Klux Klan men) and then it's a rush for buses and taxis back to Home on the Range, wherever that may be.

The Grand Old Opry (there's one in Nashville, too, I am told) was set up in an old cinema on Paisley Road – the PR, as it is known – to cater for the strong engagement with Americana amongst a section of Glasgow society. Those attending are clearly working class, though there is the odd example of radical chic amongst the audience which finds its way across the river from the West End. There is a roguish outlaw element in the Glasgow working man (and woman), and possibly the tales told in the songs of cowboys, hillbillies and hobos appeal to that element. I walk away, the lone figure, hoping I look like a mysterious drifter, The Man in the Long Black Coat of Dylan's ballad, and head home.

The area around the Opry and the Paisley Road Toll is the interface between Kinning Park to the west and Kingston to the east, and represents a striking contrast between the motorway and its environs, which smashed an old working-class tenement community, and a set of garish American style cinemas and other places of entertainment lying towards the river. In amongst the planning blight stand the empty ruins of former large factories; Dunn's bakery, Howden's engineering works, and isolated jewels like Mackintosh's Scotland Street School.

I walk home through this area, and crossing the Millennium (aka Squinty) Bridge I pause, spotting another Glasgow icon: the last of the paddle steamers, the *Waverley,* sitting at its new berth beside the futuristic Science Centre and the Glasgow Eye. In the days when these paddle steamers were the mainstay of working-class holidays, they always had music on board. They also were exempt from most alcohol restrictions; hence the appellation 'steaming' became synonymous with being drunk. A different set of people seek musical interest on the *Waverley:* more 'respectable' working class – less outlaw than the Grand Old Opry clientele – and more affluent. The Opry is still less than a fiver for entry, while a trip on the Waverley will cost you well over £20. Musical tastes on the boat are different too, and tend towards Jazz rather than Country and Western, in a venue played in the 1950s by Glasgow's most famous jazz band, The Clyde Valley Stompers.

In summer the boat frequently has jazz bands on board to entertain the customers, and there is also the annual Jazz Cruise from the Broomielaw during the Jazz Festival. This can be an entertaining event, sailing Doon the Watter on (hopefully) a fine evening, enjoying the view. Once punters could see the bustling industrial sites on the riverside where they worked, but then, as this industry was lost, the river became a sad and almost dead place. Today there is once again a flurry of human activity, made possible by the construction of flats and the building of new museums and tourist attractions. Amongst the desolation and decay stand the new Riverside Museum on the site of a former shipyard, the luxury high flats at Meadowside where there was once a granary, the huge shopping centre at Braehead, and the former Yarrow's shipyard, still working as BAE Systems and producing warships for the Royal Navy. Well wrapped up against the breeze, the braver passengers gather at the bow of the ship on the way downstream, following the visual narrative provided by the river.

At the Tail of the Bank there are fine views of the Cowal Hills, but at the turning things get more serious. Punters hasten below out of the cooling evening air and start the business of consuming fish suppers, copious amounts of alcohol, and dancing to the music in whatever space is available, be it alleyways, decks, or tables. I recall on one occasion watching the sweat pouring off the dancers and hearing a communication from the captain to the effect that, as all the passengers were to one side of the boat, one of the *Waverley*'s paddles had come out of the water and the vessel could only go in circles: would they please spread themselves around the vessel more evenly to aid safe navigation?

Glasgow was recently awarded the title by UNESCO of City of Music (just as Edinburgh was awarded the accolade City of Literature). I wonder if this was in part for what goes on at the Opry and on the *Waverley*, or whether these things even made it onto UNESCO's radar. They should. Despite the Opry being short of new recruits and the Waverley being short of funds, their musical events are part of the culture of the city, though probably not providing the income for Glasgow that other more prominent strands of its musical life do. What is a cultural icon, after all? The Kelvingrove Dali's *Christ* surely, the collection of Mackintoshiana obviously, but let me make a plea for the Grand Old Opry, though it may never gain Arts Council funding, and for the *Waverley* as well.

The image of the *Waverley*, one of the last working examples of the engineering skills for which the Clyde was once famous, sailing down the river into the sunset may be a fitting one with which to end this book, which has taken us on a journey through some of the rich and varied iconography bequeathed to us from the industrial era in a city which itself stands as an icon of that whole historical epoch.

Luath Press Limited
committed to publishing well written books worth reading

LUATH PRESS takes its name from Robert Burns, whose little collie Luath (*Gael.*, swift or nimble) tripped up Jean Armour at a wedding and gave him the chance to speak to the woman who was to be his wife and the abiding love of his life. Burns called one of 'The Twa Dogs' Luath after Cuchullin's hunting dog in Ossian's *Fingal*. Luath Press was established in 1981 in the heart of Burns country, and now resides a few steps up the road from Burns' first lodgings on Edinburgh's Royal Mile.
Luath offers you distinctive writing with a hint of unexpected pleasures.

Most bookshops in the UK, the US, Canada, Australia, New Zealand and parts of Europe either carry our books in stock or can order them for you. To order direct from us, please send a £sterling cheque, postal order, international money order or your credit card details (number, address of cardholder and expiry date) to us at the address below. Please add post and packing as follows: UK – £1.00 per delivery address; overseas surface mail – £2.50 per delivery address; overseas airmail – £3.50 for the first book to each delivery address, plus £1.00 for each additional book by airmail to the same address. If your order is a gift, we will happily enclose your card or message at no extra charge.

Luath Press Limited
543/2 Castlehill
The Royal Mile
Edinburgh EH1 2ND
Scotland
Telephone: 0131 225 4326 (24 hours)
Fax: 0131 225 4324
email: sales@luath.co.uk
Website: www.luath.co.uk